The Olympus Book

FOCAL CAMERA BOOKS

THE ASAHI PENTAX BOOK	*Clyde Reynolds*
THE ASAHI PENTAX BOOK, K RANGE	*Clyde Reynolds*
THE MINOLTA XE-1 & SR-T BOOK	*Clyde Reynolds*
THE NIKON F & F2 BOOK	*Clyde Reynolds*
THE NIKKORMAT BOOK	*Clyde Reynolds*
THE OLYMPUS OM-2 & OM-1 BOOK	*Leonard Gaunt*
THE PRAKTICA BOOK	*Leonard Gaunt*
THE ZORKI & FED BOOK	*Leonard Gaunt*

FOCAL CAMERA GUIDES

ASAHI PENTAX GUIDE 18th ed.	*W. D. Emanuel*
BOLEX H8 H16 GUIDE 9th ed.	*A. J. Surgenor*
CANNONET GUIDE 5th ed.	*W. D. Emanuel*
CANNON REFLEX GUIDE 4th ed.	*W. D. Emanuel*
EXAKTA 35 mm GUIDE 10th ed.	*W. D. Emanuel*
HASSELBLAD GUIDE 4th ed.	*W. D. Emanuel*
KONICA COMPACT 35 mm GUIDE 1st ed.	*W. D. Emanuel*
KONICA REFLEX GUIDE 6th ed.	*W. D. Emanuel*
LEICA GUIDE 44th ed.	*W. D. Emanuel*
LEICAFLEX GUIDE 4th ed.	*A. Matheson*
MAMIYA SEKOR SLR GUIDE 3rd ed.	*W. D. Emanuel*
MINOLTA SR GUIDE 9th ed.	*W. D. Emanuel*
MINOX GUIDE 8th ed.	*W. D. Emanuel*
MIRANDA GUIDE 2nd ed.	*W. D. Emanuel*
NIKON F GUIDE 5th ed.	*W. D. Emanuel*
NIKKORMAT GUIDE 6th ed.	*W. D. Emanuel*
OLYMPUS OM-1 GUIDE 2nd ed.	*W. D. Emanuel*
OLYMPUS 35 mm COMPACT GUIDE 2nd. ed.	*W. D. Emanuel*
PRAKTICA PRAKTICAMAT GUIDE 8th ed.	*W. D. Emanuel*
RETINA GUIDE 24th ed.	*W. D. Emanuel*
RETINA REFLEX GUIDE 6th ed.	*W. D. Emanuel*
RETINETTE GUIDE 8th ed.	*W. D. Emanuel*
ROLLEICORD GUIDE 7th ed.	*W. D. Emanuel*
ROLLEIFLEX GUIDE 39th ed.	*W. D. Emanuel*
ROLLEI 35 mm GUIDE 2nd ed.	*W. D. Emanuel*
YASHICA GUIDE 7th ed.	*W. D. Emanuel*
YASHICA 35 mm GUIDE 4th ed.	*W. D. Emanuel*

CAMERA WAY BOOKS

THE ASAHI PENTAX WAY 9th ed.	*Herbert Keppler*
THE CANON REFLEX WAY 2nd ed.	*Leonard Gaunt*
THE HASSELBLAD WAY 6th ed.	*H. Freytag*
THE LEICA & LEICAFLEX WAY 11th ed.	*Andrew Matheson*
THE NIKON/NIKKORMAT WAY 1st ed.	*Herbert Keppler*
THE PRAKTICA WAY 3rd ed.	*Leonard Gaunt*
THE RETINA WAY 10th ed.	*O. R. Croy*
THE ROLLEI WAY 9th ed.	*L. A. Mannheim*
THE ROLLEIFLEX SL66 & SLX WAY 1st ed.	*L. A. Mannheim*

THE OLYMPUS BOOK

for OM1 and OM2 users

LEONARD GAUNT

FOCAL PRESS

London and New York

ISBN 0 240 50942 0

First Edition 1977

Printed and bound in Great Britain at The Pitman Press, Bath

Contents

Where to look for . . .

Single-lens reflex features

In a single-lens reflex camera the viewfinder image is formed by the camera lens. Thus, the viewfinder image is always the same, allowing for framing tolerances, as that which subsequently appears on the negative or slide. No separate viewfinder is necessary when the camera lens is changed or when attachments such as close-up lenses, extension tubes, bellows or tele-extenders are used.

In the older single-lens reflexes, this principle was simply achieved by placing a movable mirror at a 45 degree angle behind the lens to redirect the image through 90 degrees to a ground glass screen in the top of the camera. The mirror was so placed that the distance from its surface to the film and to the viewfinder screen were the same. Thus, the viewfinder screen could also be used for focusing. When the image was accurately focused on the screen it must also be in focus on the film.

Later refinements

This is still the basic principle that is used in the modern 35 mm single-lens reflex, although many refinements have been added. The 35 mm camera for example is nearly always used at eye level so an ingenious five-sided prism (pentaprism) was designed to sit on top of the focusing screen to turn the image-forming rays through another 90 degrees so that the user could look in the direction of the subject while he took his picture. But that is not all the pentaprism does. It also corrects the lateral reversal that would be present if simple mirrors were used, so that the viewer sees an upright, right-way-round image on his screen.

The final part of the 35 mm single-lens reflex viewing system is the eyepiece lens, focused on the viewfinder screen via the reflecting surfaces of the prism. This is a magnifying eyepiece which enables the viewer to see an image that appears nearly life size when the standard 50 mm lens is attached to the camera.

The 35 mm single-lens reflex

TOP
1   Subject
2   Lens
3   Diaphragm
4   Viewing and focusing screen
5   Pentaprism
6   Viewfinder eyepiece
7   Pressure plate
8   Mirror
9   Film
10   Image as seen through eyepiece

BOTTOM
The film used in the 35 mm single-lens reflex is 35 mm wide, perforated along both edges. The image size is normally 36 x 24 mm and generally includes fractionally more than is visible in the viewfinder.

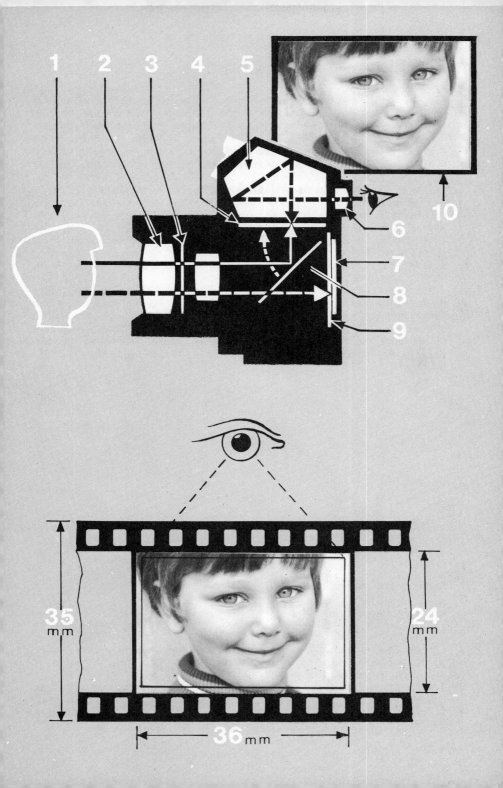

Single-lens reflex operation

The main refinements that have been added to the original single-lens reflex design are the instant return mirror and the automatic diaphragm. Early cameras of this type were rather slow in operation and a little disconcerting to the user. Although the mirror automatically flipped up out of the light path when the shutter release was pressed, it stayed there, blacking out the view through the eyepiece until the film was wound on for the next exposure – an operation that also tensioned the shutter.

Similarly, as it is always advisable to view and focus the image at its brightest, the user had constantly to open and close the lens diaphragm between shots. Inevitably, he frequently forgot to stop down after focusing and overexposed his film by shooting unintentionally at full aperture.

The modern single lens reflex overcomes both of these problems. The mirror not only rises automatically just before the shutter opens but also returns to the viewing position when the shutter closes. The viewfinder blackout is barely noticeable at the faster shutter speeds.

The diaphragm setting problem was overcome by linking the operation with a simple push rod or sliding lever mechanism emerging from the back of the lens mount. Pushing the pin inward or the lever sideways closes diaphragm down, either by direct action or by releasing a spring mechanism in the lens. Thus, a simple link in the camera body connected to the shutter release stops down the lens automatically while the shutter is open and lets it return to full aperture when the shutter closed.

Sequence of operations

The complete single lens reflex operation is:

1   The picture is composed and focused on the viewfinder screen with the mirror down and the lens at full aperture.
2   The aperture control ring is set to the required shooting aperture and the shutter release depressed. The lens diaphragm stops down to the pre-set aperture, the mirror rises and the shutter opens.
3   The shutter closes, the mirror returns to the viewing position and the lens diaphragm returns to the fully open position. The pre-set aperture remains and when the shutter release is pressed again, the diaphragm again stops down to that aperture.

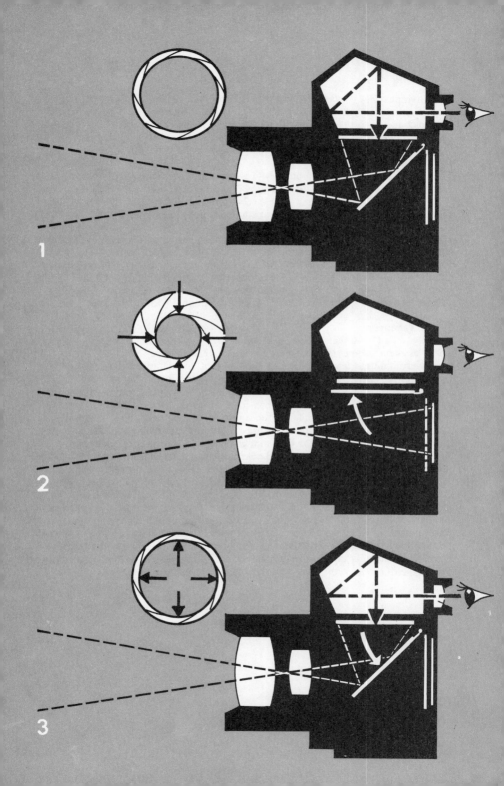

1

2

3

Olympus OM-1 and OM-2

The Olympus OM-1 was introduced in 1972 as the first of a new breed of small lightweight single lens reflex cameras. The original models could be modified by Olympus agents to take a motor drive (see page 76) but subsequent export models had the motor drive connections factory fitted.

OM-1 features
The main feature of the Olympus OM-1 was its then exceptional compactness and light weight. The body measures 786 × 83 × 50 mm and weighs 490 g (17.3 oz). With the heaviest standard lens – the f 1.2 – it weighs 800 g (28.2 oz). It is a 35 mm single-lens reflex taking 35 mm film in standard cassettes and giving pictures 36 × 24 mm. It has a fixed pentaprism, but interchangeable viewfinder screens (see page 68). Among the unusual features are the film speed setting dial in the position more commonly occupied by the shutter speed dial. Shutter speeds on the OM-1 are set on a ring on the front of the camera body around the exclusive OM bayonet lens mount. The metering system is of the full-aperture type, reading through the lens via two cadmium sulphide (Cds) light sensors.

In most other aspects the camera is a conventional SLR of its type.

OM-2 features
The Olympus OM-2 was first seen at the 1974 Photokina and began to appear on world markets in late 1975. It bears a strong resemblance to the OM-1 but has many very different features. Despite the fact that it is an automatic-exposure version, it has the same body dimensions as the OM-1 and is only slightly heavier. The few external differences are mostly confined to the film speed setting dial and the meter system on-off switch, which has four positions on the OM-2.

The metering system is similar to those devised and patented by the Minolta and Canon companies, reading the exposure required in the automatic mode from a special reflective pattern on the first shutter blind and, during long exposures, from the film surface. This system avoids the Asahi-patented methods using memory circuits to store the meter reading after the mirror rises. Manual operation is possible, but not without a battery in the camera and the switch set to manual; because the shutter is totally electronically controlled and cannot operate without a battery.

The metering system is of the aperture-preferred type (you set the aperture and the meter sets the shutter speed), but you can set approximately the shutter speed you want by adjusting the aperture until the speed required shows in the viewfinder. Automatically measured exposures cover the range from 1/1000 sec to 60 secs. An interesting feature is that in the automatic mode, the meter is actually a stopped-down type, although you can view the readout at full aperture.

Olympus OM-1 and OM-2
Externally, the cameras show only minor differences: A, OM-2. B, OM-1.

Olympus OM-1

With the introduction of the Olympus OM-1 in 1972, the Olympus Optical Co claimed a reduction of 35 per cent in volume compared with the average SLR and a similar reduction in weight. This was achieved, they claimed, by radically redesigning the whole camera and its accompanying system.

The redesigning is largely internal and is not evident from the outside. The camera, apart from its small size and weight, is a conventional 35 mm SLR with full-aperture TTL metering and all the normal functions of a camera of its type.

Viewfinder
The immediately obvious difference is the large viewfinder image, which means, in fact, that this small camera actually has a larger-than-usual viewfinder screen combined with wide-angle viewfinder optics. The result is an image about 30 per cent greater than in most other 35 mm SLRs.

The finder shows about 97 per cent of the actual picture field and contains additionally only a central rangefinder spot and the exposure meter needle. Magnification is 0.92X at infinity with a 50 mm lens. The mirror is an oversize type to avoid viewfinder vignetting with lenses up to 800 mm and can be locked up.

Shutter
The shutter is a more or less conventional cloth focal plane type but has nylon strings instead of the more usual tapes as a space saving device. It has the normal range of speeds from 1-1/1000 sec, plus a B setting and has both X and FP synchronisation, changed by a switch around the coaxial socket. There is also a hot-shoe socket in the pentaprism into which an accessory shoe with cableless contact can be screwed. A self-timer allows a 4-12 sec delay on the shutter release.

Film advance is by conventional lever with a ratcheted action allowing operation by a single stroke or by several short strokes. The action also tensions the shutter, operates the frame counter and sets the double exposure prevention device. The counter indicates the number of frames exposed and returns to zero when the camera back is opened.

Accessories
Accessories include a full range of lenses from 8-1000 mm focal length, including zoom, macro and shift lenses. There are many accessories for macrophotography and photomicrography as well as the motor drive and 250-exposure back.

Olympus OM-1 features

1	Frame counter	15	Distance scale
2	Film-speed-dial release button	16	Lens release button
3	Film transport lever	17	Carrying strap lug
4	Film speed dial	18	Self timer
5	Shutter release	19	Rewind release
6	Viewfinder eyepiece	20	Mirror lock
7	Hot shoe socket	21	Flash socket and switch
8	Shutter speed ring	22	Lens
9	Meter switch	23	Battery compartment
10	Rewind crank	24	Motor-drive guide-pin hole
11	Rewind knob/back release	25	Motor-drive coupling
12	Depth-of-field scale	26	Tripod socket
13	Focusing ring	27	Motor-drive contacts
14	Aperture ring		

Olympus OM-1

With the f1.8 standard lens, the Olympus OM-1 measures 81 mm from front to back. The f1.2 lens adds 16 mm, bringing the depth to 97 mm, while the f1.4 provides an intermediate 86 mm. All the standard lenses have a minimum focusing distance of 45 cm ($17\frac{3}{4}$ in). The f1.8 and f1.4 have 49 mm filter threads for front--of-lens attachments and the f1.2 lens has a 55 mm thread.

The back of the OM-1 hinges to the right and can be opened fully on releasing the latch by pulling firmly upward on the rewind knob. It is self-latching when pressed shut. The back can be completely removed to allow the Recordata Back or 250 Film Back to be attached.

Eyepiece attachments

Viewfinder eyepiece attachments include a soft rubber eyecup with provision for eyesight correction lenses, a combined angle finder and magnifier and a coupler both for photomicrography and to allow the eyecup to be attached when the 250 Film Back is in use.

The interior of the back is orthodox with dual sprockets for 35mm film, full-length film guide rails and polished runners. The film is loaded by threading its leader into the slotted take-up spool. There is no easy-load facility.

Olympus OM-1 features

1	Shutter speed ring	10	Rewind knob/back release
2	Aperture ring	11	Film chamber
3	Mirror lock	12	Film guide rails
4	Shutter speed ring grip	13	Viewfinder eyepiece
5	Depth-of-field preview	14	Shutter blind
6	Lens release button	15	Sprocketed spindle
7	Flash socket with switch	16	Take up chamber
8	Shutter-speed-ring grip	17	Removable hinge
9	Focusing ring	18	Camera back

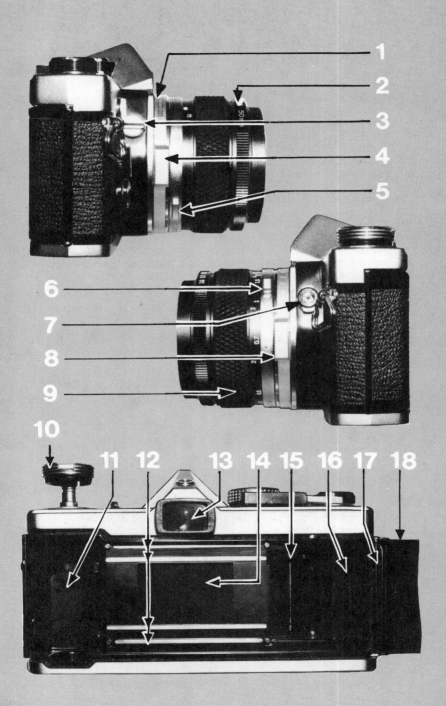

Olympus OM-2

Continuing the tradition of the OM-1, the Olympus Optical Co introduced the OM-2 as the smallest camera of its type in 1975/6. It is an automatic-exposure 35 mm single lens reflex with TTL metering. The dimensions of the camera are exactly the same as those of the OM-1 − 136 × 83 × 50 mm without lens.

Metering system
The metering system is unique. It uses two CdS sensors, as in the OM-1, to give an estimate of the shutter speed that will be set by the meter and timed by the electronically-controlled shutter. Additionally, it has two silicon blue sensors reading the light reflected by the first shutter blind and, on long exposures, by the film. These control the actual shutter speed set in the automatic mode. The CdS sensors alone indicate the shutter speed which you should set in the manual mode.

Viewfinder
The viewfinder is basically the same as that of the OM-1 and the screens are interchangeable. The OM-2 finder, however, has a more complicated readout. The needle indicates the shutter speed which will be set in the automatic mode or acts as a centering needle in the manual mode. When the meter is switched off, only the tip of the needle is visible in the bottom left hand corner of the screen. The other readouts are removed.

Accessories
The OM-2 takes the same range of lenses and accessories as the OM-1 plus an electronic flash unit for automatic operation via the sensors in the camera. A remote sensor is also available.

Olympus OM-2 features

1	Frame counter	15	Lens release button
2	Film transport lever	16	Shutter speed ring
3	Film speed setting	17	Self timer
4	Exposure compensation	18	Rewind release
5	Viewfinder eyepiece	19	Shutter release
6	Auto flash connection	20	Flash socket and switch
7	Hot-shoe contact	21	Lens
8	Meter switch	22	Carrying strap ring
9	Rewind crank	23	Battery compartment
10	Rewind knob/back release	24	Motor-drive guide-pin hole
11	Depth-of-field scale	25	Motor-drive coupling
12	Focusing ring	26	Reset button
13	Aperture ring	27	Tripod socket
14	Distance scale	28	Motor-drive contacts

Olympus OM-2

With the same dimensions as the OM-1 and with virtually identical mechanical functions, the OM-2 does, nevertheless, have detail differences that are apparent in these side and back illustrations.

The back opens from right to left, as on the OM-1, and its latch is released by pulling the rewind knob upward. It is completely removable if necessary (to fit the 250 or Recordata Backs) and is self latching when pressed shut. The difference here is the film reminder slot, designed to take the end of the film carton to remind you what film you have loaded.

The other difference in the back view is that the OM-2 has a battery check light to the left of the viewfinder eyepiece, brought into operation by the meter switch.

The right-hand side view shows a notable omission, because the OM-2 has, unaccountably, no mirror lock. The left-hand side view shows an addition – the reset button necessary to reset the shutter mechanism if batteries fail or the shutter is released with no batteries in the camera.

The eyepiece is similar to that on the OM-1 and takes the same accessories. It is, however, slightly redesigned and more recessed than on the earlier OM-1 models.

The interior is the same as the OM-1, with no differences in loading or film transport.

Olympus OM-2 features

1	Shutter speed ring	7	Shutter-speed-ring grip
2	Aperture ring	8	Reset button
3	Focusing ring	9	Film reminder
4	Depth-of-field preview	10	Battery check light
5	Lens release button	11	Viewfinder eyepiece
6	Flash socket with switch		

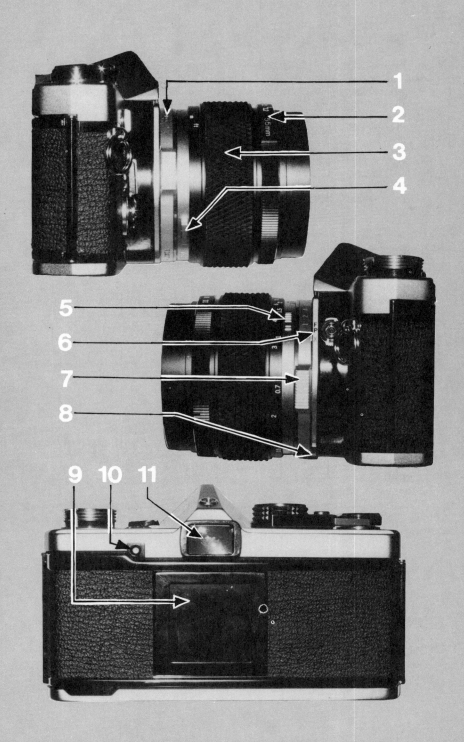

Olympus OM system

The Olympus OM cameras are part of an extensive system of equipment, not all of which can be dealt with in detail in this book. The system ranges from a lens cap to a 46-piece collection of macrophotographic equipment. The equipment available falls broadly into five groups: Lenses, Motor Drive, Close-ups, Macrophotography and Photomicrography.

Lenses
The lenses range from 8 mm and 16 mm fisheyes to a 1000 mm super telephoto, including a 75-150 mm zoom. They all have automatic diaphragms and all the long-focus lenses are of compact telephoto construction. There are four macro lenses, including an auto diaphragm type that also focuses to infinity. The others focus via the Auto Bellows and have manual diaphragms, as has the Shift lens.

Motor Drive
The motor drive group includes an extremely small motor drive unit with power pack and 250 exposure back, AC power source and a bulk film loader.

Close-ups
Close-up photography is well catered for by two types of copy stand and a small-subject macrophoto stand, plus close-up lenses and extension tubes.

Macrophotography
For macrophotography proper, there is the extensive Macrophoto Equipment PMT-35, as well as the Auto Bellows with double cable release, three bellows-fitting macro lenses, a focusing rail and stage and a variety of lighting units and other equipment.

Photomicrography
The photomicrography group, not covered in detail, is a highly specialised range of equipment, as might be expected from a manufacturer of high-quality microscopes and other laboratory equipment. There are two basic systems: the PM-1-A with the automatic exposure body PM-PBA and the PM-10-M with manual exposure body PM-PBM. The automatic system compensates for reciprocity-law failure over a wide range of exposure times.

The group includes many accessories, such as a photomicrographic exposure meter, focusing telescope and magnifier, a special supporting stand, eyepiece adapters, etc.

Other items
Additional accessories include flash units, Recordata Back, interchangeable screens, Varimagni Finder, filters, close-up lenses, extension tubes, eyecup and eyepiece correction lenses and many other items.

Olympus accessories
A, Varimagni Finder. B, Dioptric correction lens. C, Eyecup. D, Accessory shoe. E, Electronic flash. F, Interchangeable screen. G, Extension tubes. H, Filter. J, Close-up lens. K, Bulb flashgun. L, Lenses. M, 250-exposure back. O, Macro-adaptor. P, Macro equipment. Q, Motor Drive. R, Motor drive power pack. S, Micro adaptor. T, Recordata Back. U, Auto Bellows.

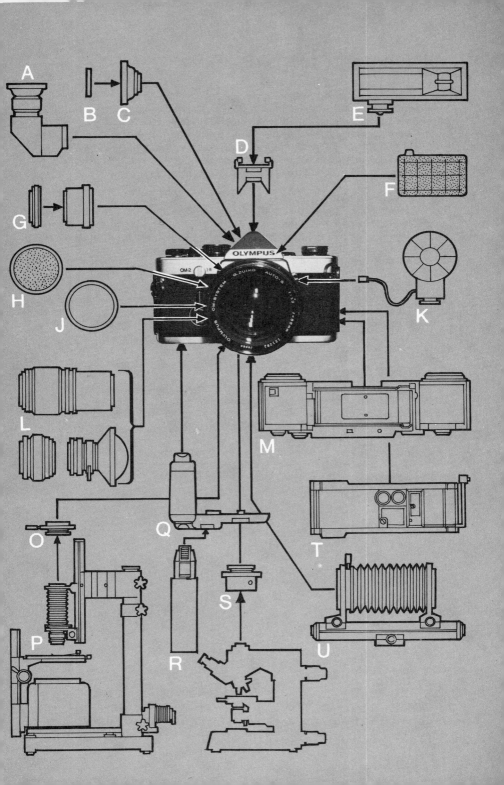

Viewing and focusing

The standard viewfinder screen of the Olympus OM cameras is a fine matt field with a central microprism rangefinder spot. The screen can be removed and replaced by one of the range of alternative screens available (see page 68).

The viewfinder image is almost life size with a 50 mm lens used at the infinity setting. The area shown is slightly less than that which appears on the film to allow for the fact that colour slide mounts and many enlarger negative carriers have apertures slightly smaller than the standard 35 mm image area.

Rangefinder focusing

The microprism spot can be used for focusing the image, which is projected on the screen by the camera lens and duplicates the image that will subsequently appear on the film. As you turn the focusing ring on the lens mount in either direction, the lens moves backward or forward to focus on farther or nearer objects respectively. To focus on a particular object or plane, you sight the object in the viewfinder and turn the focusing ring until the image appears perfectly sharp.

The image in the central microprism spot is broken and shimmering when the lens is not accurately focused, but steadies and sharpens as correct focus is achieved. This method is unreliable, however, at lens apertures smaller than f 4, when the microprism area may become darker and far less precise than the matt field of the rest of the screen. Olympus supply interchangeable focusing screens for this very purpose (see page 68).

Full-aperture focusing

Generally speaking, focusing at full aperture is always preferable because depth of field (see page 128) is then least and the image moves quickly in and out of focus as the setting of the lens focusing ring is varied. As all the normal lenses for the Olympus OM cameras have automatic diaphragms that do not stop down until the shutter release is pressed, focusing at full aperture is the normal procedure.

Apart from the microprism centre, the OM-1 viewfinder has no other features or readouts except the exposure meter needle and its index marks. The OM-2 readout changes according to the position of the meter switch.

Viewfinder features

1   Matt field   2   Rangefinder

As you turn the focusing ring toward the correct object distance (3), the broken image in the rangefinder area (4) becomes clear and sharp (5).

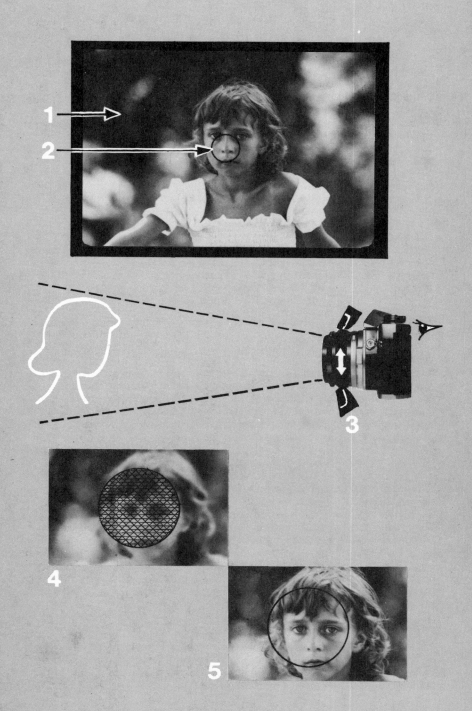

Exposure controls

To obtain an image of a subject on film, you have to expose the film to the light rays reflected by that subject and focused on the film. The amount of light reaching the film varies with the amount of light reflected by the subject. That, in turn, varies with the strength of the light falling on the subject and the efficiency with which the subject reflects that light.

The film needs a certain amount of light to form a satisfactory image – the actual amount depending on the sensitivity or speed of the film (see page 94). Thus, we need controls to match the light reflected from the subject to the sensitivity of the film. The camera allows us to use both time and intensity in this way (*top*).

To control the length of time for which the light is allowed to act on the film, we can vary the shutter speed.

To control the intensity of the light that is allowed to act on the film, we can obscure part of the lens by means of a variable aperture or stop.

Shutter operation

On the Olympus OM cameras the shutter can be set to give automatically timed exposures from 1 to 1/1000 second or manually controlled exposures of any duration by setting the shutter speed ring to B. The automatic speeds double up in the sequence

$$1000 \quad 500 \quad 250 \quad 125 \quad 60 \quad 30 \quad 15 \quad 8 \quad 4 \quad 2 \quad 1$$

These figures are the denominators of the appropriate fractions of a second, 125 indicating 1/125 second, etc.

Aperture settings

Similarly, the intensity of the light can be varied in doubling or halving steps by obscuring more or less of the lens rather in the manner of drawing curtains across a window (*bottom*). Camera lenses, however, have diaphragms consisting of metal leaves forming a continuously variable, more or less circular opening. The diaphragm is controlled by an aperture ring on the lens with click stops at specific, marked positions. These markings are in the sequence

$$1 \quad 1.4 \quad 2 \quad 2.8 \quad 4 \quad 5.6 \quad 8 \quad 11 \quad 16 \quad 22 \quad 32$$

and are known as *f*-numbers or relative apertures.

For each lens, the ends of the scale vary, some stopping at 16 and perhaps starting at intermediate figures such as 1.8, 3.5 etc.

The standard markings, however, follow the doubling-up principle because they are calculated by dividing the focal length of the lens by the effective aperture – which is the diameter, at each aperture setting, of the light beam striking the front surface of the lens and passing through the hole in the diaphragm (the limiting aperture). And to double the light-transmitting ability of a circular hole, you need to double its area, which amounts to multiplying its diameter by $\sqrt{2}$. Allowing for a certain amount of rounding off for convenience, the above sequence follows that principle.

Exposure controls

Exposure is the product of time (shutter speed) and intensity (aperture). For a given film speed in given lighting conditions, there is one such product to provide correct exposure, but it can be obtained by various settings of the camera controls.

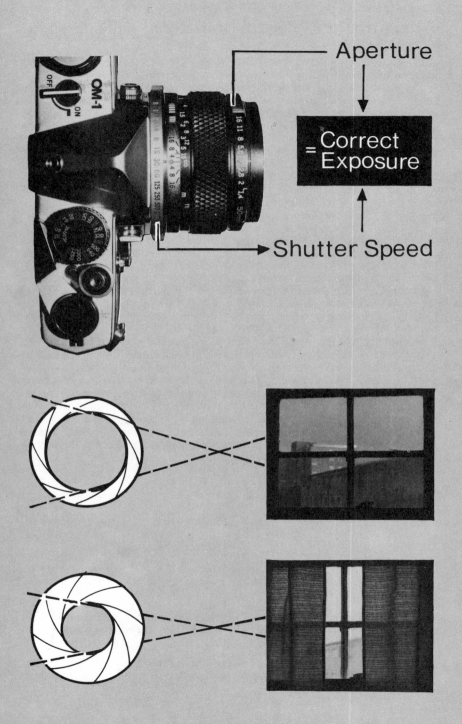

Aperture

= Correct Exposure

Shutter Speed

Aperture and depth of field

Although used primarily to control the exposure (with the shutter speed) the lens aperture has a further effect on the final picture. It determines how much of the subject is recorded sharply. Anything exactly at the focused distance is rendered absolutely sharp, provided there is no camera or subject movement. However, closer objects and those farther away will theoretically be not quite as sharp. In practice, there is always a zone of sharp focus from somewhere in front of the subject to somewhere behind it. This is called the depth of field, and its magnitude is determined by the lens aperture and the focused distance.The larger the aperture (smaller the f-number), the smaller the depth of field for a particular lens, and also the closer the focused distance, the smaller the depth.

It is not actually the f-number, but the effective aperture (see p. 26) which determines the depth of field. Thus, the depth (at any given focused distance) for a 50 mm lens at f5.6 is the same as that for a 200 mm lens at f22. Of course, the depth of field for a 200 mm lens at f5.6 is much smaller.

The depth of field may be seen through the viewfinder if the lens is stopped down to the selected aperture by pressing the stop-down button on the lens. Depth of field may, alternatively, be read from the scale on the lens barrel. When the lens is focused, the limits of sharp focus are indicated on the distance scale by the two marks corresponding to the selected f-number. There is not room to engrave marks for all the possible apertures, so some are left out. You have to interpolate between the lines for the missing aperture settings. The small red dot indicates the infrared focusing mark (see p. 50).

A small depth of field may be used to creative purpose – for example to make a sharply focused subject stand out against a soft background. This is achieved by choosing a large lens aperture (e.g. f4 on a 50 mm lens). In other circumstances, as small an aperture as practical (e.g. f16) must be chosen to render as much as possible of the subject sharp. The greatest usable depth is obtained by focusing neither on the foreground subject, nor on the background, but somewhere in between. For distant subjects set the depth-of-field calibration for your chosen aperture against the infinity (∞) mark. The focused distance is then called the hyperfocal distance for that aperture. The closest sharp focus (indicated by the other calibration for the same f-number) is half the hyperfocal distance.

Depth of field

TOP The lens distance scale is used in conjunction with the depth of field scale to estimate depth of field. The distances appearing against the f-numbers at which you shoot indicate the near and far limits.

BOTTOM For a visual indication, you can check the view on the screen after stopping down the lens to the preselected aperture by pressing the stop-down button.

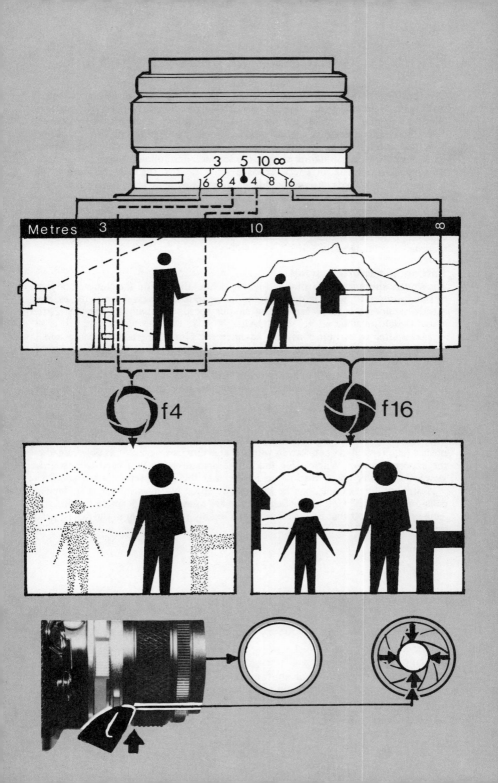

Metres   3   10   ∞

f4

f16

Shutter operation and speed settings

Olympus OM cameras are fitted with focal plane shutters. The shutter is located within the camera body as close as possible to the film. It consists of two fabric blinds on rollers. The rollers are tensioned when you wind on the film. When you press the shutter release one blind starts to move horizontally across the camera back and is followed by the other after an interval which depends on the shutter speed set. At the faster shutter speeds, the second blind follows the first very quickly, so that the film is, in effect, exposed strip by strip through the narrow gap between the two blinds. At slower shutter speeds, the delay before the second blind is released is greater and the gap between the blinds is correspondingly larger. As the actual speed of traverse of the blinds remains constant, there comes a time when the gap has to be as wide as the image format. This, in fact, occurs at a speed setting of about 1/60 sec. At that and all slower shutter speed settings, the whole image is recorded simultaneously.

Setting the shutter speed
The shutter speed is set by rotating the ring behind the lens on the camera body until the appropriate figure is opposite the index spot. Settings between the marked speeds cannot be used. When setting shutter speeds manually on the OM-2, the meter switch must be set to MANUAL.

The shutter is tensioned as you advance the film after each exposure and is released by pressing the shutter release knob on the camera top plate, either directly or by means of a cable release. Long exposures can be given by setting the shutter speed ring to B. The shutter then remains open as long as you hold the release button down. To set the OM-2 shutter to B, hold the reset button in while turning the shutter speed ring.

Subject movement
The shutter speed you set depends primarily on the nature of the subject and exposure requirements in connection with the aperture (see page 26) as determined by the exposure meter. When using the OM-2 on automatic you need to check the viewfinder shutter speed readout to ensure that the speed set suits the subject.

A still life, for example, can be shot at any speed but even moderate movement calls for a speed of 1/60 sec or faster if you are to avoid blur. Rapidly moving subjects or any subject that might move unpredictably must be shot at the fastest practicable speed.

Shutter speed and subject

TOP
Provided the camera is adequately supported, a still life can be shot at slow speeds.

MIDDLE
Moving subjects need faster shutter speeds. Even 1/60 sec is relatively slow when the subject is fast moving and you get a blurred result.

BOTTOM
To freeze fast movement, you need the fastest possible shutter speed.

Loading the camera

To load an Olympus OM camera, first open the camera back by pulling the rewind knob firmly upward. It offers a little resistance before the back springs open. Open the back fully to the right.

Insert a loaded 35 mm film cassette in the film chamber below the rewind knob and push the knob back, twisting it as necessary to lower it fully into position. Pull the film leader out of the cassette and lay it across the camera back between the film guide pins. Insert the tip of the leader into one of the slots in the take-up spool beneath the film transport lever.

Holding the cassette in place with the left thumb, operate the film transport lever to draw the film out of the cassette. Check that it moves evenly across the camera back and that the sprocket teeth on the spindle beside the take-up spool engage in the film perforations on both edges. Fold down the camera back and press it firmly so that it locks shut.

Fold out the rewind crank and turn it gently clockwise to take up the slack film in the cassette. Stop turning when you meet firm resistance.

Setting film speed

Set the film speed. The procedure varies according to model. On the OM-1, first pull the film transport lever slightly away from the camera body. Press the dial release button next to the shutter release and turn the film speed dial until the appropriate figure appears opposite the line on the collar around the shutter release. Make sure that the dial does not move when you let go the release button.

On the OM-2, lift up the outer rim of the exposure compensation dial located next to the shutter release and turn it until the appropriate film speed figure appears in the cut out on the top of the dial. Let the rim drop back and check the setting. Turn the dial until the white line is opposite the black line on the pentaprism housing. You can turn the ring of the compensation dial only through three stops. If you have to turn it further, release the rim when you feel resistance and turn the dial in the opposite direction. Then lift the outer rim again and turn to the required setting.

Finally, transport the film and depress the shutter release. Repeat until the figure 1 appears in the frame counter. As you use the camera the frame counter adds one for each shot you take. It runs from 1 to 36 plus S for start and E for end. These letters and the numbers 12, 20 and 36 (standard cassette loadings) are marked in gold. The counter resets to S when the camera back is opened.

Loading the OM-1 and OM-2

1 Unlock camera back
2 Insert loaded cassette
3 Push down rewind knob
4 Insert film leader in take-up spool
5 Transport film
6 Check sprocket drive
7 Close camera back
8 Take up film slack
9 Set film speed
10 Transport film to wind off exposed leader

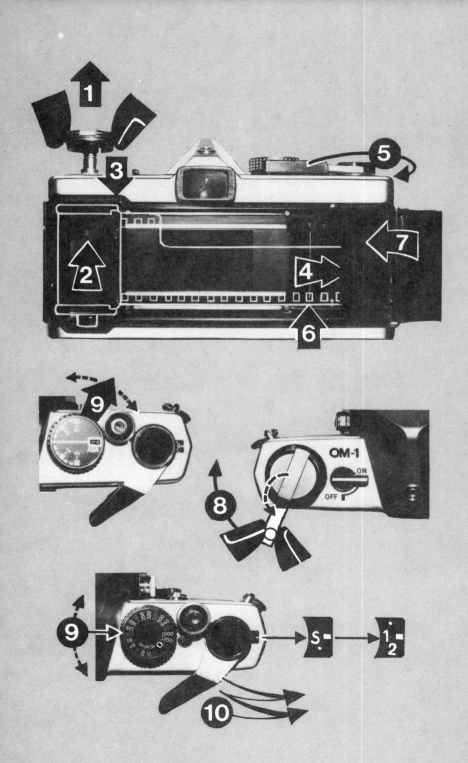

Using the OM-2 exposure meter

The OM-2 exposure meter is a dual-function type. It can be used either in the manual mode, when you set both aperture and shutter speed by adjusting either or both until the needle in the viewfinder is centred; or it can be left to select a suitable shutter speed after you have set the aperture.

The second method is the one for which the camera is primarily designed. When you set the exposure meter switch to AUTO, a shutter speed scale from 1000 to 1 appears in the viewfinder, representing shutter speeds from 1/1000 sec to 1 sec. Additionally a red zone appears at the top of the scale to indicate that, at the aperture and film speed set, you would need an exposure shorter than 1/1000 sec. A blue zone at the bottom with the word AUTO indicates that the shutter speed set will be longer than 1 sec (up to 60 secs). The blue figures on the scale are simply an indication of shutter speeds sufficiently slow to warrant particular care in supporting the camera.

Automatic operation

To operate the camera in the auto mode, you turn the meter switch to AUTO, set the aperture you require, frame and focus your subject, and press the shutter release. The shutter speed actually used approximates to that shown by the needle in the viewfinder, which is activated by the CdS sensors on either side of the eyepiece. The actual speed may be slightly different because it is governed by the silicon blue sensors at the front of the mirror box. At speeds faster than 1/60 sec, they measure the light reflected from the reflective pattern on the shutter blind. At speeds of 1/60 sec and slower, the reading is taken partly from the shutter blind and partly from the film surface.

Even in the auto mode, you can, of course, select any shutter speed you require (from 1/1000 sec to 1 sec) by turning the aperture ring until the required shutter speed is indicated in the viewfinder. You can also compensate for non-average subjects (see page 36).

Manual operation

In the manual mode, the meter operates on the normal centre-needle principle. Turn the meter switch to MANUAL. The shutter speed scale disappears and you are left with the two index marks and exposure compensation marks. Compose and focus your picture and then set the aperture you require and adjust the shutter speed (or vice versa) until the needle is centred between the index marks. The camera is then set for correct exposure. In the manual mode metering is effected entirely by the CdS sensors. The SBCs play no part in this procedure. For exposure compensation procedure, see page 36.

Using the exposure meter

1 Check that you have set the correct film speed
2 Switch to AUTO or
2A Switch to MANUAL
3 For auto operation, set aperture
3A For manual operation, set aperture or shutter speed
4 Check needle position in viewfinder. If speed unsuitable, change aperture
4A For manual operation, adjust aperture or shutter speed to centre needle

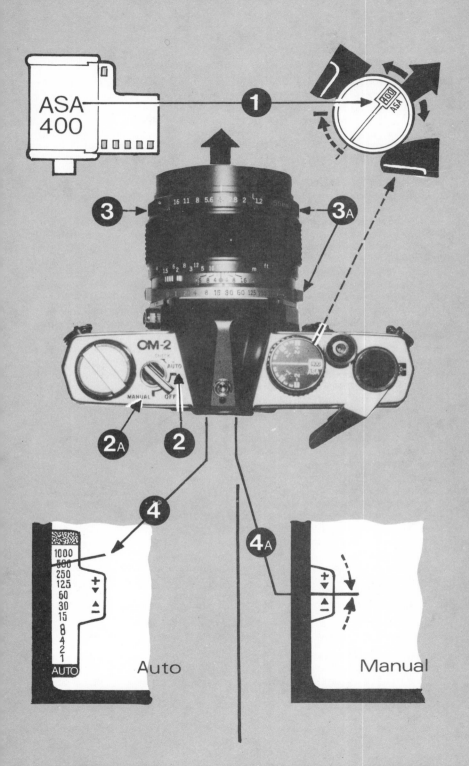

ASA 400

OM-2

Auto

Manual

Exposure compensation

Any exposure meter has to work on simple principles. It has to assume that whatever it reads is a mid-tone or a collection of tones that averages out to a mid-tone (see page 116). Naturally, there are some subjects that are not composed of such a collection of tones. There are, for example, backlit subjects where the background might be a brilliant sky or backcloth that far outweighs the light reflected from your main subject. On the other hand, your main subject may be light while the background is dark.

How the meter is misled

In these circumstances, any meter can be misled. If it reads a predominantly light scene, it assumes that you want the picture to average out to a mid-tone. So the dark subject against a light background is given too little exposure and conversely the light-toned subject against a dark background is given too much exposure. This, of course, assumes that the background occupies by far the greater part of the picture.

When the whole subject is predominantly light-toned, a normal meter reading tends to underexpose it. When it is all dark, it may be overexposed. In either case, you end up with a mid-toned result.

The Olympus OM-2 has an exposure compensation control to enable the automatic exposure device to cope with such unusual subjects. In the normal automatic mode (see page 34), you turn the white line on the exposure compensation dial to the black index line on the pentaprism housing. When you encounter a rather light-toned subject or one that is strongly backlit or side lit so that the meter is likely to give a too optimistic reading, turn the dial to bring +1 or +2 opposite the index. The +2 setting is rarely necessary – probably only with a really brilliant background such as strongly reflecting water or when a strong light source is in the picture area.

When the subject is predominantly dark-toned or is light-toned against a very dark background, a straight meter reading tends to overexpose it. Turn the exposure compensation dial to bring −1 opposite the index. The −2 setting is needed only in extreme cases.

Alternative method

An alternative procedure is to approach the subject closely (or zoom in on it, or change to a longer-focus lens) and read an area that is to be reproduced as a mid-tone. Note the shutter speed indicated, return to your shooting position or focal length and turn the exposure compensation dial until that shutter speed is indicated in the viewfinder.

When using the OM-2 manually, you can obtain similar results by adjusting the aperture and/or shutter speed until the needle moves to the minus (for less exposure) or plus (for more exposure) index marks.

A similar procedure for the OM-1 is described on page 38.

Compensating for the unusual subject

The exposure compensation dial on the OM-2 enables you to reset the meter for unusually lit subjects. In effect, you alter the film speed rating. In the manual mode, you simply adjust the exposure settings to place the needle off centre.

The OM-1 has a similar control more fully described on page 38.

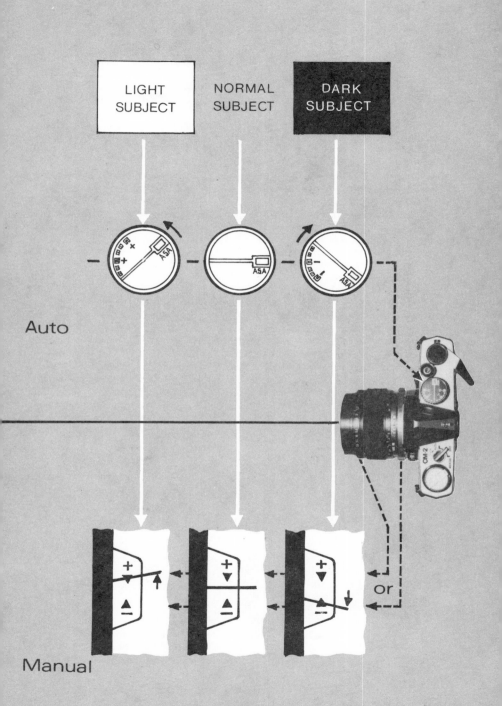

LIGHT SUBJECT

NORMAL SUBJECT

DARK SUBJECT

Auto

Manual

or

Using the OM-1 exposure meter

The exposure meter of the Olympus OM-1 camera is an orthodox CdS full-aperture type, reading the screen illumination (commonly referred to somewhat inaccurately as reading through the lens) by means of sensors on either side of the viewfinder eyepiece. It is coupled to the aperture and shutter controls and the film speed setting. It has a switch on the camera top plate next to the rewind knob. When the switch is set to OFF or when the light level is too low for the meter to measure, the needle is removed from the viewfinder.

Normal procedure
To use the meter for normal subjects, first check that the film speed has been correctly set (see page 32). Turn the meter switch to ON, frame and focus the picture in the viewfinder and select either the aperture or shutter speed at which you wish to shoot. This decision can be governed by depth-of-field considerations for aperture (see page 28) or subject movement for shutter speed (see page 26). Note the position of the needle in the viewfinder. It should be centred in the index. If it is not, adjust the aperture or shutter speed settings until it is. If you cannot centre the needle at your chosen aperture or shutter speed, correct exposure is impossible at that setting and you have to alter it. If the needle does not move at all, the battery is incorrectly loaded or is exhausted (see page 52).

Exposure compensation
When the needle is centred, the camera controls are set for correct exposure of a subject with a normal distribution of tones, i.e. averaging out to a mid-tone (see page 116). If the subject has an unusual distribution of tones, you need to give rather less or more exposure than the meter indicates. For a predominantly dark subject, for example, the meter tends to recommend too much exposure. If you set the needle off-centre toward the minus mark you can give half a stop or a stop less exposure than when the needle is centred. To give more exposure, set the needle toward the plus mark.

Using the OM-1 meter

1	Check film speed setting		speed to centre needle
2	Switch meter on	**5**	For subjects with unusual tone
3, 3A	Set shutter speed or aperture according to subject		distribution, set needle off centre for more or less
4, 4A	Set aperture or shutter		exposure

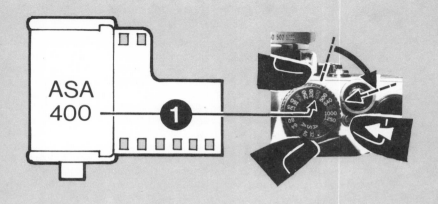

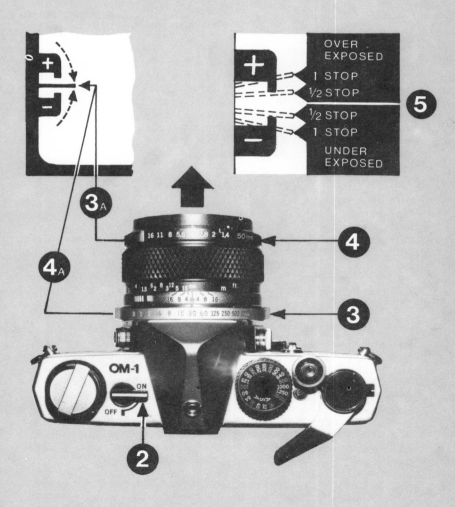

OVER
EXPOSED

1 STOP
1/2 STOP
1/2 STOP
1 STOP

UNDER
EXPOSED

Stopped-down metering

The automatic diaphragm lenses for the Olympus OM cameras have a meter coupling lever protruding from the back of the lens mount. This lever moves as the lens aperture ring is adjusted and alters the setting of the meter circuit within the camera to allow it to take account of the shooting aperture when making its measurement through the full aperture of the lens. Naturally, this operation can take place only when the lens is directly attached to the camera body.

Thus, when an automatic lens is used in conjunction with extension tubes or bellows, it can no longer connect with the exposure meter and cannot be used for full-aperture metering. In these circumstances, therefore, the OM cameras have to be used in the stopped-down metering mode. The meter is set for stop-down operation by the bellows itself, by the extension tubes (which are not auto-diaphragm types) or by any other Olympus item without meter coupling pin, such as the Zuiko Shift lens. Stopped-down metering is, of course, nothing new for the OM-2 in the auto mode, because it always meters at the shooting aperture. However, the CdS sensors (for the display) must be set in the same way by a manual accessory.

Manual operation

With the OM-1, or for manual operation of the OM-2, the the procedure is generally to set the aperture first, after switching on the meter. In close range work, depth of field is restricted and subject movement is not generally a problem, so the aperture is normally of more importance than the shutter speed.

With the aperture set, press the stop-down button on the lens mount, except when using any of the special Olympus macro lenses for bellows mounting, and, with the subject properly framed and focused, adjust the shutter speed to centre the needle in the viewfinder index. When using the Shift lens or if you have a close-range subject that might show some movement (such as a live insect) you may need to set the shutter speed first. You may do so but remember to press the stop-down button as you adjust the aperture to centre the needle.

Automatic operation

When using the OM-2 in the auto mode, you set the aperture in the normal way and allow the meter circuit to set the shutter speed.

The actual shooting operation with either model when using an auto diaphragm lens then calls for the use of a double cable release (see page 72) if you are to avoid holding the stop down button while releasing the shutter.

A close-range subject is quite likely to need exposure compensation. Follow the procedure on pages 36 and 38.

Stopped-down metering

The OM full-aperture metering system cannot work unless the lens is directly attached to the camera. The attachment of any Olympus equipment without meter coupling lever (such as A, Shift lens. B, bellows. C, extension tubes) sets the meter for stopped-down operation. The OM-2 meter then works normally with the meter switch set to AUTO or MANUAL.

With the OM-1 meter switched on or the OM-2 meter switched to MANUAL:

  1 Set aperture, generally to provide required depth of field
  2 Press stop-down button if using auto-diaphragm lens
  3, 4 Adjust shutter speed to centre needle

Use a double cable release to shoot if lens has auto diaphragm.

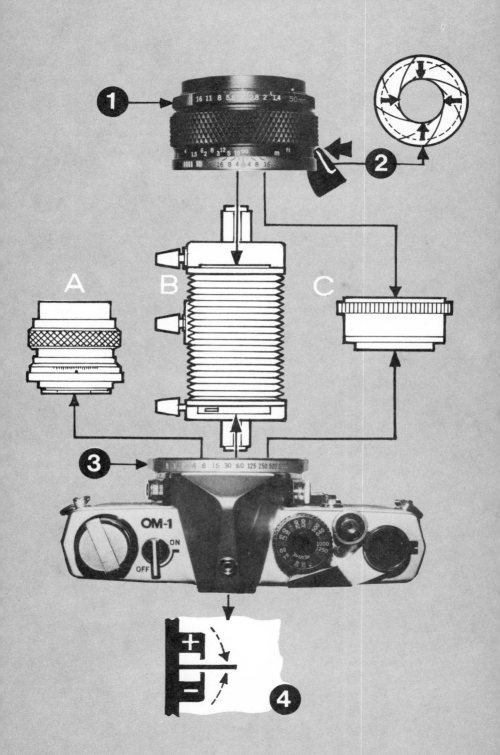

Holding the camera

One of the most common causes of unsharp pictures is camera shake, i.e. movement of the camera during exposure. While the picture is being taken, an image of the subject is projected by the lens on to the film. If the camera moves, even imperceptibly, while the shutter is open, the image is displaced on the film and forms a double or multiple image. In most cases, the movement is so fractional that the different images are indistinguishable. The result is, however, a thickening of fine lines and an enlargement of small detail, producing an image less sharp than the camera is capable of producing.

Thus, every precaution must be taken at all times to hold the camera completely still – even when using the fastest shutter speeds. At slower speeds the risk of movement is naturally greater but blur induced by camera shake is possible even at 1/1000 sec.

Generally, the steadiest hold is provided when the photographer stands straight, with the legs slightly apart and the weight distributed equally on each leg. The camera should be held firmly but not too tightly in both hands with the arms against the sides and elbows well in.

Horizontal and vertical holds

The easiest grip for horizontal pictures is as shown opposite. The left hand operates focusing, shutter speed and aperture controls as well as the meter switch. The right hand winds on the film and releases the shutter.

The grip for vertical pictures can be as shown, with the first or second finger of the right hand releasing the shutter, or the hands can be reversed with the camera the other way up and the thumb on the release button.

Always take advantage of any support that may be available by resting the camera or the elbows on a wall, chairback, etc. or by leaning against a tree, lamppost or other support, or even by lying prone and propping the elbows on the ground. Sometimes you may be able to place the camera on a convenient support and let the self-timer (see page 50) release the shutter.

Remember that it needs only a fractional displacement of the image to produce unsharp pictures. Therefore, the narrower angle of view of longer focal length lenses can induce blur with considerably less camera movement than if a shorter focus lens were used.

The camera must be absolutely steady for sharp pictures

Camera shake is the enemy of truly sharp pictures. Cultivate an easy stance and steady hold so that the camera can be held perfectly still at the moment of exposure.

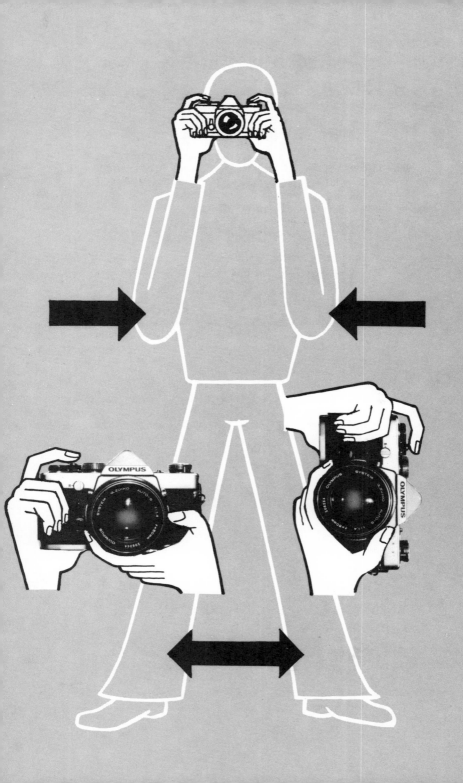

Shooting with the OM-1

Having loaded the camera and set the film speed you are ready to take pictures. It is advisable to standardise your procedure so that you become used to it and do not forget part of the operation and miss a vital picture. A recommended sequence is as follows, although you can, of course, make minor variations to suit your own methods.

First, as the exposure meter is battery-powered, switch on the meter with the switch next to the rewind knob. Check that the film has been wound on by attempting to move the film transport lever fully to the right. Decide whether you wish to shoot at a particular aperture or shutter speed and set either accordingly.

Looking through the viewfinder eyepiece, compose the picture on the screen and focus sharply.

Check the position of the exposure meter needle. For most general photography, it should be centred in the index claw. If it is not, adjust the aperture or shutter speed until it is (see page 38). Aperture and shutter speed are then set for correct exposure and you can press the shutter release to take the picture.

Wind the film on again ready for the next exposure and switch off the meter.

Varying the procedure

The variations possible are concerned mainly with the meter operation. You can, of course, switch on at any time up to taking the reading and you may not switch off if you are taking a sequence of pictures. On the other hand, if your sequence is of similar subjects in constant lighting conditions, there is no point in taking a fresh reading each time. Provided your first reading is correctly taken, you can switch off immediately and use the same exposure for subsequent shots. Even if you change the shutter speed you can make a compensating change of aperture or vice versa without taking a fresh reading.

It is also a matter of preference whether you wind on the film immediately after the exposure or wait until you are ready for the next shot.

Shooting sequence — OM-1

1	Remove lens cap	6	Set shutter speed to centre needle
2	Switch on meter		
3	Compose and focus picture	7	Release shutter
4	Check meter needle	8	Transport film
5	Set aperture	9	Switch off meter

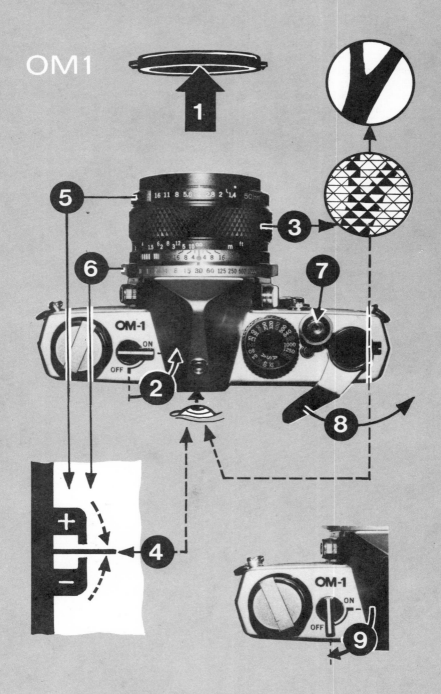

OM1

Shooting with the OM-2

The OM-2 offers two methods of shooting because it can be operated either manually or automatically. The procedure is broadly the same as with the OM-1 and offers more or less the same options, in that you can follow your own preferred operating methods. It is as well, however, to standardise on a particular sequence to ensure that you know exactly what you are doing at all times.

Manual operation

In the manual mode, the camera is virtually an OM-1, with full-aperture metering via the CdS sensors in the pentaprism housing. In the automatic mode the SBC sensors in the bottom of the camera come into use and the camera is a stopped-down reading type with full-aperture readout.

To operate manually, therefore, you switch the meter to MANUAL, compose and focus your picture and set aperture and shutter speed as required, ensuring that the meter needle is centred in the index.

Automatic operation

To operate automatically, set the meter switch to AUTO, focus and compose your picture and set the aperture as required. Check the readout in the viewfinder where the CdS sensors cause the needle to indicate the approximate shutter speed that the SBC sensors will set when you press the shutter release. If the speed is unsuitable, adjust the aperture setting to provide the shutter speed you require.

In either case, the camera controls are now set for correct exposure and you can press the shutter release to take the picture. With the exposure completed, transport the film and switch off the meter.

Shooting sequence – OM-2

1	Remove lens cap	**5A**	Adjust aperture or
2	Switch on meter		shutter speed to centre
3	Compose and focus picture		needle
4	(Auto) Set aperture	**6**	Release shutter
4A	(Manual) Set aperture and	**7**	Transport film
	shutter speed	**8**	Switch off meter
5	Check shutter speed		

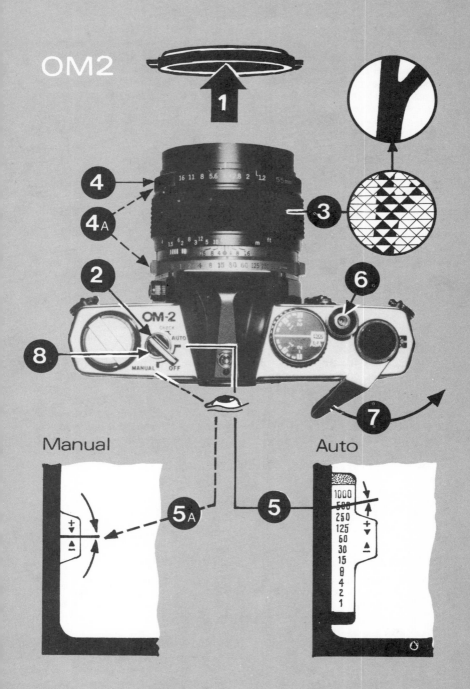

OM2

Manual

Auto

Unloading: Multiple exposures

The frame counter beside the film transport lever normally indicates the number of the next frame to be exposed. So, when it indicates the number of frames you have loaded into the camera, you know you have one more shot to take before you have to reload. The numbers 12, 20 and 36 are gold-coloured to distinguish them, because they are the commonly available packings. If you load your own cassettes from bulk film, you can load any number of frames up to 36.

After making the last exposure on the roll, set the camera for rewinding by turning the rewind release lever on the camera front until the red line is opposite the R. This allows the sprocketed spindle to run freely. Fold out the rewind crank from the rewind knob and turn it clockwise until you feel a slight increase in tension as the film pulls away from the take-up spool. The crank then turns easily as the film leader is wound into the cassette.

You can then open the rear cover by pulling the rewind knob upward and remove the cassette from the camera.

Making multiple exposures

Like most modern cameras, the Olympus OMs have a double-exposure-prevention device. Once you have operated the film transport lever, you cannot move it again until after you release the shutter. Similarly, once you have released the shutter, you cannot open it again until it is retensioned, which you do by winding on the film. There is no specific provision for multiple exposures on the same frame on the OM cameras but you can do it with some manual dexterity.

After taking the first of your two (or series) of shots that are to appear on the same frame, take up any slack in the cassette by turning the rewind knob gently in a clockwise direction until you feel the film offering heavy resistance. Keep hold of the rewind knob and do not let it slip back. Turn the rewind release lever to the R position and hold it. Now operate the film transport lever to tension the shutter and make your next exposure. You need to practise the manoeuvre with an empty camera to decide which fingers to employ for each operation. The point of the exercise is that you must hold on to both the rewind knob and the rewind release lever throughout to prevent the film from moving while you tension the shutter. You can repeat the operation as often as you wish but do not expect to obtain perfect register.

The frame counter adds one for each exposure even though the film does not advance.

Unloading procedure

1 Set rewind release lever to R.
2 Rewind film
3 Open back
4 Remove cassette
5 Close back

Multiple exposures

1 After the first exposure, take up slack in cassette and hold rewind knob
2 Set rewind release lever to R and hold it
3 Tension shutter
4 Frame picture and release shutter

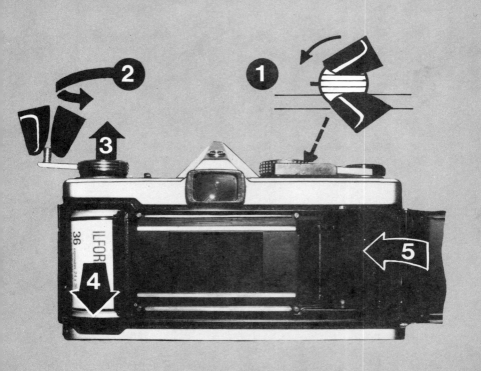

Additional features

Among the additional useful features on the Olympus OM cameras are a self-timer, and infra red focusing mark and a removable back cover.

Self-timer
The OM self-timer is in the orthodox position on the camera front beside the lens. To actuate it, pull the lever sideways and down away from the lens until it points vertically downward. You can do this before or after winding on the film but make sure that you do wind on (and so tension the shutter) before releasing the self-timer. To release, push the smaller lever now uncovered toward the lens. The timer mechanism starts to run and releases the shutter after 12 seconds. If you change your mind, you can release the shutter before the 12 seconds in the normal way or stop the timer by turning the small lever back away from the lens.

The timer does not function if the film has not been wound on. The lever stops in mid-travel and you have to switch it off with the small lever, return the timer lever to its original position, wind on the film and start again.

For shorter delay times (down to about 4 seconds) do not move the lever so far. The timer can work from any position lower than about midway through its travel.

Infra red focusing mark
When shooting on infra-red sensitive film, it is usual to place an opaque or deep red filter over your lens. You cannot then see the image clearly enough to focus accurately. The OM lenses therefore have a small red mark to the right of the normal focusing index on the depth of field scale. To use it, you focus on your subject without the filter and then move the distance scale to bring the indicated subject distance opposite the red IR focusing index. The lens is then focused for the usual type of infra red work.

Removable back
The back cover of the OM cameras is hinged to allow normal loading and un-loading operations. It can, however, be completely removed to allow the Recordata Back or the 250 Film Back to be attached to the camera.

To remove the back, press down on the small pin toward the top of the hinge. The top part of the hinge is then released and the back can be lifted clear.

To replace the back, hold the hinge pin down, insert the bottom pin into its socket, align the top and release the hinge pin.

Additional features

A Self-timer. 1, The timer is set by folding the lever downward through 180 degrees. 2, The timer is released by pushing the release lever toward the lens B Infra red focusing mark. C Removable back and Recordata Back.

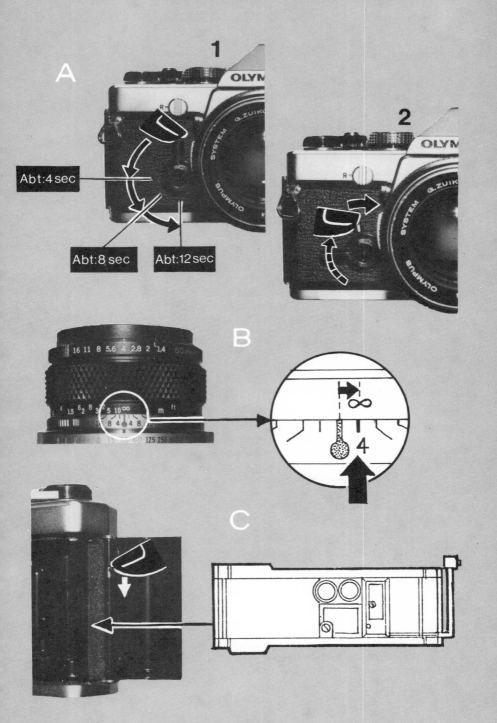

Abt:4 sec
Abt:8 sec
Abt:12 sec

Additional features

Apart from the special attachments for photomicrography, there are three main attachments for the viewfinder eyepiece of the OM cameras; the Eyecup, which also takes eyesight correction lenses, the Varimagni (angle) Finder and the Eyecoupler.

Eyecup
Spectacle users in particular find a soft rubber eyecup not only more comfortable in use but also less damaging to their spectacles than the unyielding rim of the viewfinder eyepiece. The Eyecup also prevents stray light entering the finder and influencing the meter reading in the stopped-down metering mode.

Dioptric correction lenses
Eyesight correction lenses can be snapped into the slot provided in the Eyecup and held by a threaded retaining ring. Corrections are obtainable from 2 to −5 dioptres.

Varimagni finder
With nine lens elements and a mirror, this is a useful combination of angle finder and magnifier with individual eyesight adjustment. The Varimagni slips into the viewfinder eyepiece, allowing the tubular section to rotate through 360 degrees so that you can view the image from any required angle. A large focusing ring on the tube allows you to adjust the optics to suit your particular eyesight. A switch on the fixed section allows you to alter the magnification from 1.2X the whole image area to 2.5X the central portion for really critical work.

Eyecoupler
The Eyecoupler is an extension piece that fits between the viewfinder eyepiece and the Varimagni finder. It is primarily intended for more convenient viewing in photomicrography but is also necessary when the 250 Film Back is used.

Mirror lock
You may want to lock the mirror up on the OM-1 in extreme close-up work or in rapid sequence shooting with the motor drive to avoid vibration. Normally the camera is rigidly supported for this work. Compose your picture and focus critically. Turn the lever on the side of the mirror box (close to the rewind release lever) counter-clockwise through about 90 degrees to a positive stop. Take your picture or pictures and immediately return the lever to its original position. It is not advisable to carry the camera around outdoors with the mirror locked up.

OM-1 battery
The OM-1 uses a single 1.3 volt mercury battery of the 625 type. It fits into the battery compartment with the plus side up. The battery will last about one year in normal use.

Eyepiece attachments

TOP
1	Rubber eyecup
2	Dioptric correction lens
3, 3A	Varimagni Finder with angular adjustment
4	Eyecoupler

OM-1 features

BOTTOM
| A | Mirror lock |
| B | Battery |

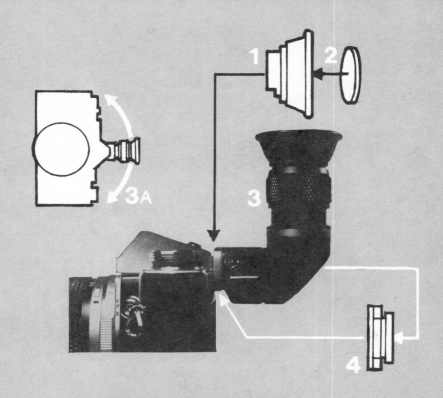

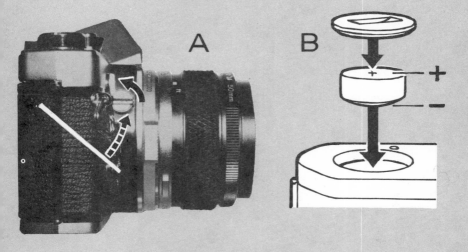

OM1

A

B
+
−

Special features — OM-2

Among the special features of the Olympus OM-2 camera are its unique metering system, a battery check facility, a reset button and a film type reminder

Metering system

In the manual mode, the OM-2 meter operates just like that of the OM-1. When you switch to AUTO, however, you bring into the meter circuit two silicon blue sensors in the camera base lined up to read the reflective pattern on the first shutter blind. The pattern is designed to give a centre-weighted reading. The meter translates the reading into a value of light intensity at the film surface and adjusts the electronic shutter to a suitable speed to give correct exposure for the film speed set. The metering and shutter speed adjustment is continuous while the shutter is open for longer exposures but then most of the reading is taken from the film surface and is not centre-weighted. Thus, the meter reading in the AUTO mode is taken at the shooting aperture. An estimate of its effect is made by the CdS sensors and is shown in the viewfinder before the shutter is released. That reading is, of course, not continuous.

Batteries

The OM-2 uses two 1.5 volt silver oxide batteries housed in the camera base. The battery compartment cover unscrews anti-clockwise. Place the batteries in the compartment with plus sides up and replace the cover. Do not handle the batteries any more than is necessary.

To check battery power, move the meter switch to CHECK. If the red lamp on the camera back shows continuously, battery voltage is sufficient. If it flashes on and off, battery voltage is low and early replacement is advisable. If no light shows, the batteries are dead.

Reset procedure

The OM-2 cannot work without batteries. If you press the shutter release when there are no batteries in the camera or the batteries are dead, the lens stops down, the mirror flips up but the shutter cannot function. Before loading new batteries, you must reset the camera. Press the reset button and turn the shutter speed ring until the reset asterisk is lined up with the red triangle on the lens mount. The mirror and shutter locks are then released.

The reset button also has to be used to set the shutter to B, which can be used only in the manual mode. Switch the meter to MANUAL, hold the reset button in and turn the shutter speed ring to B. The shutter can then be held open for as long as you keep the shutter release depressed.

Film type reminder

The film type reminder slot in the back of the camera is designed to take the torn-off end of a film carton so that you always know the type of film loaded into the camera.

OM-2 special features

A Auto-metering system	D Reset button
B Loading batteries	E Film type reminder
C Battery check	

OM2

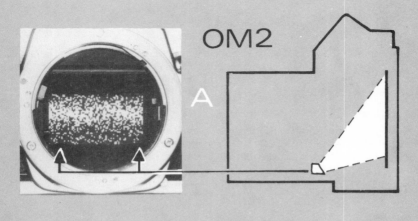

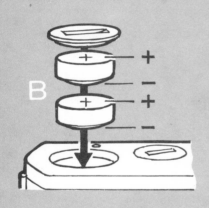

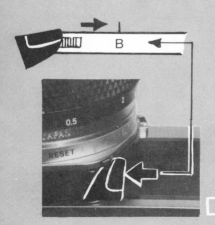

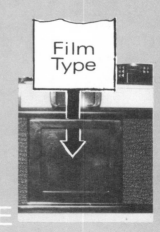

Film Type

Flash synchronisation

The Olympus OM-1 and OM-2 are identically synchronised for flash, but the OM-2 has the additional facility of automatic-exposure flash via a special accessory shoe and flash unit and its normal automatic-exposure metering system. When using any other flash equipment, set the OM-2 shutter to MANUAL.

FP setting
Both cameras have a flash synchronisation switch around the coaxial socket on the mirror box wall at the rewind end of the camera. The switch has two positions – FP and X. The FP setting is for use with special long-burning focal plane bulbs, which allow the faster shutter speeds to be used. As the film is uncovered only partially at any particular instant during exposures faster than 1/60 sec, the faster burning flashbulbs and the even faster electronic flash cannot be used.

X setting
The X setting of the switch is primarily for electronic flash, which fires almost immediately the switch is closed (when the first blind reaches the end of its travel). Flashbulbs can be used on this setting but their slower burning characteristics make it advisable not to use them at speeds faster than 1/15 sec, whereas electronic flash can be used at 1/60 sec. Focal plane bulbs can be used at slower speeds on the X setting, too, but there seems little point to it. They are expensive.

Attaching the unit
The on-camera flash seating on the Olympus OM cameras is in the form of a detachable accessory shoe that screws into the socket on top of the pentaprism. To attach the accessory shoe, plug it into the socket and turn the toothed wheel in the direction of the arrow. Any cordless unit can then be mounted in the shoe to synchronise through the contact in its foot. Units with cord connection can be plugged into the socket on the side of the mirror box.

Set the switch around the flash socket to X for electronic flash or any flashbulb except the FP type. Set to FP for focal plane bulbs only.

Automatic flash exposure
The Olympus Quick Auto 310 electronic flash unit can be attached to the Olympus OM-2 by means of the special Accessory Shoe 2. It has a guide number of 34 (metres) for 100 ASA and covers up to 85 degrees horizontal or 55 degrees vertical. It uses the camera sensors for fully automatic operation, thus allowing any aperture to be used, and facilitating close range work, varying the flash duration from 1/1000 to 1/40 000 sec.

A separate sensor allows the flash to be used off camera.

Flash synchronisation

Flash units can be attached to the camera via the screw-in accessory shoe for direct contact or cable connection. Synchronisation can be switched to FP or X.

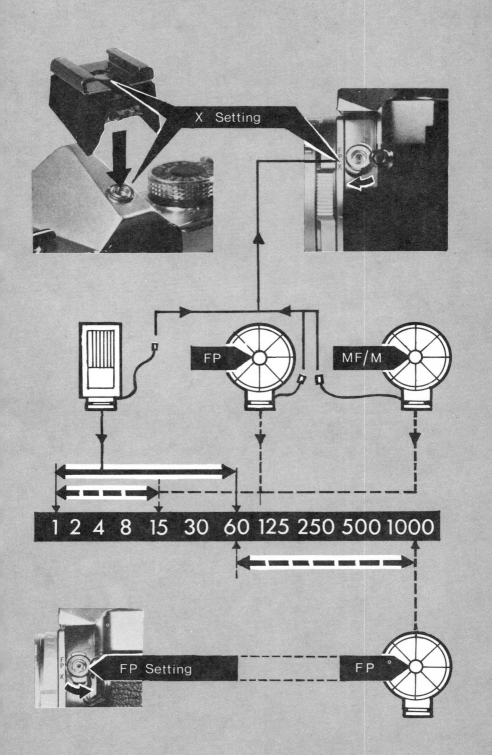

X Setting

FP

MF/M

1 2 4 8 15 30 60 125 250 500 1000

FP Setting

FP °

Fisheye and zoom lenses

Fisheye lenses produce distorted images. They have to because there is no other way they could cover a full 180 degrees. The Zuiko fisheyes use the equisolid angle projection method, which is useful for scientists and others who need to calculate the cubical angle of the image. For the ordinary photographer they produce excessively bent versions of straight lines while covering an enormous field. Your greatest difficulty in using them is to keep your hands, feet and other parts of your anatomy out of the picture.

Auto fisheye 8 mm and 16 mm

There are two versions of the Zuiko fisheye – one that places the entire image within a circle of 23 mm diameter on the film and the other that pictures a 24 by 36 mm rectangle from a large circular image. The focal lengths are 8mm and 16 mm respectively.

The 8 mm Auto-Fisheye has a maximum aperture of f 2.8 and stops down to f 22. It has 11 elements in 7 groups, focusing down to 0.2 m (7.9 in). It weighs 680 g (23.8 oz) and is 72 mm (2.8 in) in length by a maximum diameter of 102mm (4 in). It has built-in skylight, yellow, red and orange filters.

The 16 mm Auto-Fisheye has a maximum aperture of f 3.5 and stops down to f 22. It has 11 elements in 8 groups and focuses down to 0.2 m (7.9 in) and is 28 mm (1.1 in) in length by 59 mm (2.3 in) diameter. It has built-in skylight, yellow and orange filters.

Auto zoom 75-150 mm

Zoom lenses have improved in recent years in image quality and have become considerably less bulky and heavy. Although it is still doubtful whether any can outperform a prime lens of comparable quality, many can certainly produce first-class images in all reasonable conditions. The Zuiko mid-range zoom, where arguably this type of lens is most valuable, is an example of the modern zoom with a relatively limited 2:1 ratio that allows lightweight, reasonably small construction. It allows tight framing of a variety of subjects from informal portraits to sporting events when it is impossible or inconvenient to change the shooting position.

The Zuiko Auto-Zoom 75-150 mm lens has a maximum aperture of f 4 and stops down to f 22. It has 15 elements in 11 groups, focusing down to 1.6 m (5 ft 3 in). The angle of view can be varied between 16 and 32 degrees. The lens weighs 400 g (14 oz) and is 115 mm (4.5 in) long by 63 mm (2.5 in) diameter.

Fisheyes and zoom

The two Zuiko fisheye lenses both take in a full 180 degrees but the 16 mm lens presents only a rectangular view from the full circle, giving 180 degrees only on the diagonal.

The 75-150 mm Zuiko Auto-Zoom has an angle of view variable between 16 and 32 degrees.

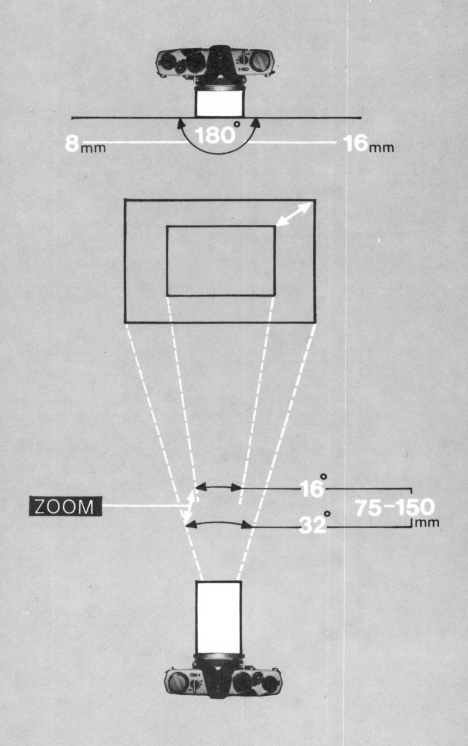

Wide angle and super wide

The Zuiko wide-angle lenses for the Olympus OM cameras range from the 18 mm super wide angle $f3.5$ to the more or less classic wide-angle 35 mm $f2$ and $f2.8$.

Wide angle lenses have become more popular as second lenses to the standard lens in recent years. This could be because better quality has been obtained from shorter focus lenses over that period. In the earlier days of the single lens reflex, plenty of wide angle lenses were available but they tended to display poor coverage in both illumination and definition at the edges of the image area. Some were also difficult to use because there was not enough room behind them for the swinging mirror to operate. The mirror had to be locked up and the reflex facility was lost.

Retrofocus design

New optical glasses and improvements in design soon led to practical retrofocus lenses in which the back focus was considerably longer than the focal length. Now, even the fisheye lenses can be used without locking up the mirror.

Lenses of 28 mm and 35 mm focal length can be considered moderate wide angles these days, especially as some photographers even prefer the 35 mm as a standard lens. They cover an appreciably larger field than the 50mm lens, allowing large or tall subjects to be shot from not too great a distance and also make it easier to shoot in crowds or small rooms. Their short focal length provides good depth of field and allows zone focusing for rapid shooting at varying distances.

The same applies, of course, to the even wider angle 24 mm and 21 mm lenses. The 24 mm may now be considered the real wide angle, covering 84 degrees and still providing good image quality. It is extremely useful for those photographers who like to stay close to their subjects and can also provide striking special effects.

Lenses for effect

The 21 mm approaches the super wide angle class and is probably more frequently used for effect than for orthodox photography. It is, nevertheless, a well-corrected lens and gives good results at close range.

The 18 mm Zuiko has an angle of 100 degrees and can provide extraordinary dramatic effects from its ability to take in large objects at close range and thus present a rapidly diminishing background that the extensive depth of field keeps in sharp focus.

Super-wide and Wide-angle lenses

Lens	Focal length (mm)	Angle (°)	Aperture Max	Min	Min. focus m	ft	Diameter mm	in	Length mm	in	Weight g	oz
L Zuiko Auto-W	18	100	3.5	16	0.2	0.65	75	2.9	42	1.6	250	8.7
G Zuiko Auto-W	21	92	3.5	16	0.2	0.65	59	2.2	31	1.2	170	6
J Zuiko Auto-W	24	83	2	16	0.25	0.82	60	2.4	49	1.9	250	8.7
I Zuiko Auto-W	24	83	2.8	16	0.25	0.82	60	2.4	36	1.4	190	6.7
I Zuiko Auto-W	28	75	2	16	0.3	1	60	2.4	43	1.7	230	8
G Zuiko Auto-W	28	75	3.5	16	0.3	1	59	2.2	31	1.2	160	5.6
H Zuiko Auto-W	35	63	2	16	0.3	1	60	2.4	42	1.6	230	8
G Zuiko Auto-W	35	63	2.8	16	0.3	1	59	2.2	33	1.3	170	6

Angles of view

The angles of view of the Zuiko wide angle and super wide angle lenses are expressed on the diagonal of the image format

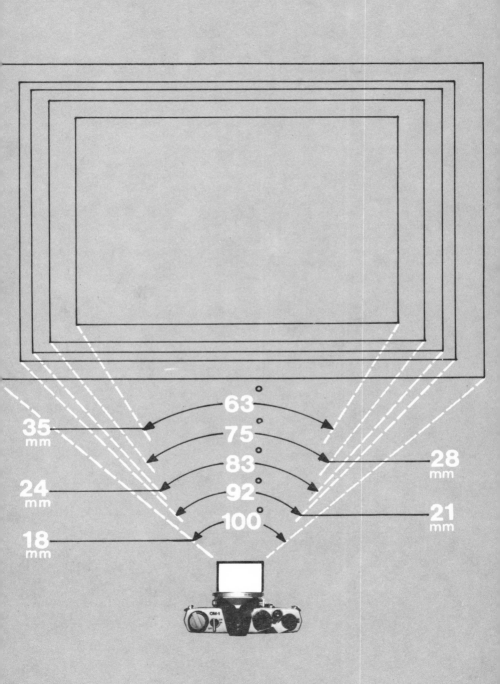

Standard and medium-long lenses

The generally accepted standard lens for a 35 mm camera has a focal length of about 50 mm. That is the lens that produces an image which, viewed from the correct distance for its degree of enlargement, presents the perspective that looks about right for normal human vision. The concept has little meaning now that cameras are so versatile. The relationship between viewing distance and degree of enlargement may, in fact, vary considerably and usually depends principally on the size of the final image. Nevertheless, lenses of 50-55 mm are labelled as standard lenses and generally offer the widest apertures available in a given range.

There are three lenses in this class for the Olympus OM cameras, including the very wide aperture 55 mm f 1.2, particularly designed for low-light work. Wide-aperture lenses tend to be bulky and, indeed, the 50 mm f 1.4 and f 1.8 Zuiko lenses are considerably smaller than the 55 mm f 1.2. Although slower, they can still be rated as fast lenses and can cope with most situations.

Telephoto construction

Depending on the type of photography you undertake, it is likely that much of your work can be carried out with a standard lens. When you work in black and white, you can enlarge part of the image only to give you the effect of a narrower angle of view. If, however, you find yourself consistently wanting to cover a smaller field, particularly in colour, you should consider buying a moderately long-focus lens in the 85-135 mm group. Long focus lenses nowadays are generally of a special telephoto construction that allows the lens barrel to be shorter than the focal length. All of the OM longer-focus lenses are of this construction.

The 85-135 mm group is particularly suited to portraiture because the larger image provided by the longer focal length enables you to shoot from a greater distance and thus avoid the possibility of perspective distortion. Naturally they are suitable in any situation where a greater shooting distance is preferable. Shots of children at play are often more easily obtained when you can stand just a few feet away from the real action so as not to distract them or get in their way.

A longer than normal lens is useful at athletics meetings when you can shoot from the trackside or relatively close to long jumpers, hammer throwers, etc. They are not a substitute, however, for getting in close and should never be used simply because you are reluctant to approach your subject closely. The greater the shooting distance the less impact action photography is likely to have, so use the long-focus lens only when really necessary.

Standard and medium long lenses

Lens	Focal length (mm)	Angle (°)	Aperture Max	Min	Min focus (m)	(ft)	Diameter (mm)	(in)	Length (mm)	(in)	Weight g	oz
F Zuiko Auto-S	50	47	1.8	16	0.45	1.5	59	2.3	31	1.2	170	6
G Zuiko Auto-S	50	47	1.4	16	0.45	1.5	60	2.3	36	1.4	230	8
G Zuiko Auto-S	55	43	1.2	16	0.45	1.5	65	2.5	47	1.8	310	10.8
G Zuiko Auto-T	85	29	2	16	0.85	2.8	60	2.3	47	1.8	230	8
E Zuiko Auto-T	100	24	2.8	22	1	3.3	60	2.3	48	1.9	230	8
E Zuiko Auto-T	135	18	2.8	22	1.5	5	61	2.4	80	3.1	350	12.2
E Zuiko Auto-T	135	18	3.5	22	1.5	5	60	2.3	73	2.8	280	9.8

Angles of view

The standard and medium long focus lenses include five focal lengths with angles of view from 47 to 18 degrees.

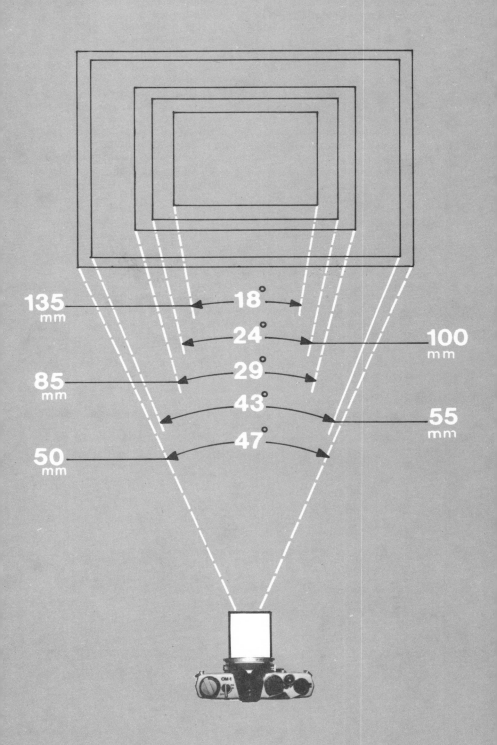

Longer-focus lenses

The most popular first choice longer-focus lens for 35 mm photographers used to be 135 mm. This is a useful lens, giving a 2.7X image magnification over the standard lens but still allowing the photographer to shoot from about 2 m (6-7 ft) when necessary. It can cover a wide range of subjects, including portraits, some sporting events, inaccessible architectural detail, many outdoor events and even some wildlife and natural history subjects.

The main reason for the 135 mm lens being the maximum that the average photographer aspired to, however, was the fact that it was about the longest lens that he could comfortably hand hold to obtain sharp images – particularly before the shorter telephoto designs became widely available. Telephotos of greater focal length still tended to be rather bulky; but that has all changed now and very compact 200 mm and even 300 mm lenses are by no means uncommon. In the Olympus range, for example, there is a 300 mm f 6.3 that is only 171 mm (little over $6\frac{1}{2}$ in) long. That is not difficult to hand hold.

Care in handling

Nevertheless, very long focus lenses have to be handled with considerable care, particularly when their rather small maximum apertures oblige you to use shutter speeds of 1/125 sec and slower. Although you may be able to hold them quite easily you cannot guarantee an absolutely shake-free hold and it needs only the tiniest movement to blur the image of a distant subject quite markedly, at least at the edges – and blurred edges make for a distinctly unsharp image. Wherever possible, lenses of 300 mm and longer should be used on a firm tripod or at least with such additional support as may be available.

As with the medium long-focus lenses, you should not use a long telephoto lens as a substitute for a closer viewpoint unless it is absolutely necessary, as in the case of timid or dangerous wildlife or at sporting or other events where you are obliged to shoot from long range.

Shooting at a distance from your subject inevitably produces perspective distortion, making even well-separated subjects look as if they are close together. Long-range shots are nearly always recognisable by the unexpectedly large scale of the background.

Longer-focus lenses

Lens	Focal length (mm)	Angle (°)	Aperture Max	Min	Min focus (m)	(ft)	Diameter (mm)	(in)	Length (mm)	(in)	Weight g	oz
E Zuiko Auto-T	200	12	4	32	2.5	8.2	67	2.6	127	5	490	17.3
F Zuiko Auto-T	200	12	5	32	2.5	8.2	63	2.5	105	4.1	360	12.7
F Zuiko Auto-T	300	8	4.5	32	3.5	11.4	80	3.1	181	7.1	1000	35.3
F Zuiko Auto-T	300	8	6.3	32	3.5	11.4	70	2.8	171	6.7	600	21.2
F Zuiko Auto-T	400	6	4.5	32	5	16.4	110	4.3	257	10.1	2200	77.6
E Zuiko Auto-T	400	6	6.3	32	5	16.4	80	3.1	255	10	1400	49.4
F Zuiko Auto-T	600	4	6.5	32	11	36	110	4.3	377	14.8	2800	98.8
E Zuiko Auto-T	1000	2.5	11	45	30	98	110	4.3	662	26	4800	170

Angles of view

There are five focal lengths in the Olympus longer-focus range, with angles of view from 12 to 2.5 degrees.

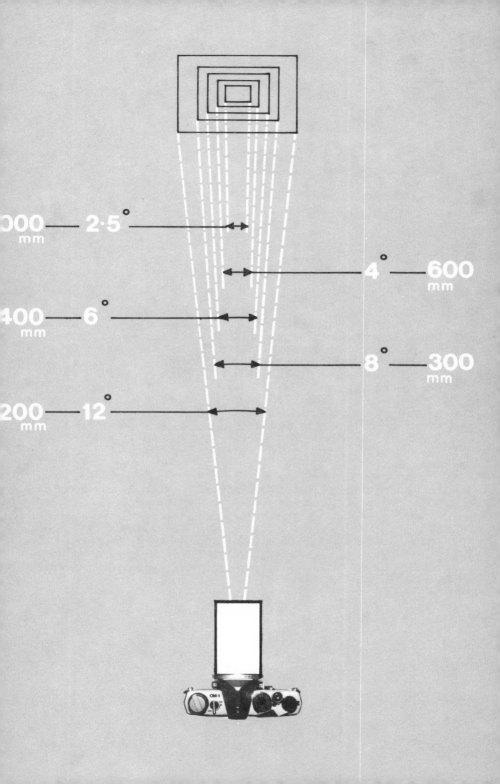

Special lenses

Among the special-use lenses for the Olympus OM cameras are the Zuiko Shift lens and four macro lenses for close-range work.

Zuiko Shift lens

One of the greatest difficulties of working with 35 mm cameras is that they are not particularly suitable for shooting very tall, very wide or regularly shaped objects with straight lines. To shoot a very tall building, you have to tilt the camera and so cause the vertical lines to converge, or use a very wide angle lens and include an unnecessarily large amount of foreground.

If you shoot a box-shaped object it is generally desirable to show two sides and the top. If, however, you raise the camera to show the top, you have to tilt it downward – and the vertical lines diverge. The same can apply in the horizontal plane, causing the horizontal lines to converge.

The shift lens overcomes these problems. It imitates some of the movements of a view camera, allowing the lens to be moved 12 mm sideways, 12 mm upward and 15 mm downward. The effect is to raise, lower or move laterally the image on the film while keeping the camera back parallel with the appropriate plane.

The Zuiko Shift lens has a focal length of 35 mm but is designed to provide an angle of coverage up to 84 degrees to make the shift usable. Its aperture range is from $f2.8$ to $f22$ and its minimum focus is 0.3 m (12 in). It has 7 elements in 8 groups. The diaphragm operation is manual. The lens weighs 350g (12.3 oz) and is 40 mm (1.6 in) long by 60 mm (2.3 in) in diameter.

Macro lenses

A weak point of most normal lenses is their inability to provide sharp images over the whole field at very close range. The precise distance at which a lens begins to show a fall-off in image quality varies from lens to lens but very few can provide edge-to-edge sharpness when the reproduction ratio reaches 1:3 or thereabouts and many cannot even approach that – even when reversed, as is often recommended for such work.

There are four special Zuiko Macro lenses to overcome these problems They are designed for specific functions. The 50 mm $f3.5$ is primarily intended for close range work at 1:2 but can also focus right out to infinity. It attaches directly to the camera and has an auto diaphragm. The other three are manual diaphragm types for use on the Auto Bellows. The 80 mm $f4$ is for 1:1 reproduction at a shooting distance of 160 mm (6 in). It covers the range from 1:2 to 2:1. The 38 mm $f3.5$ lens covers the range from 1.8:1 to 6:1, while the 20 mm $f3.5$ goes from 4:1 to 12:1. The latter two lenses need a special adaptor to enable them to be mounted on the bellows.

Zuiko Macro lenses

Lens	Min Aperture	Min Focus m	ft	Subject area Max mm	Min	Focusing	Length mm	in	Diameter mm	in	Weight g	oz
20mm f3.5	16	0.13	0.4	5 X 8	2 X 3	bellows	20	0.8	26	1.0	50	1.8
38mm f3.5	16	0.16	0.5	13 X 20	4 X 6	bellows	28	1.1	37	1.5	70	2.5
80mm f4	22	0.35	1.1	48 X 72	12 X 18	bellows	46	1.8	59	2.3	200	7.1
50mm f3.5	22	0.23	0.8	inf X	48 X 72	focusing ring	40	1.6	60	2.4	200	7.1

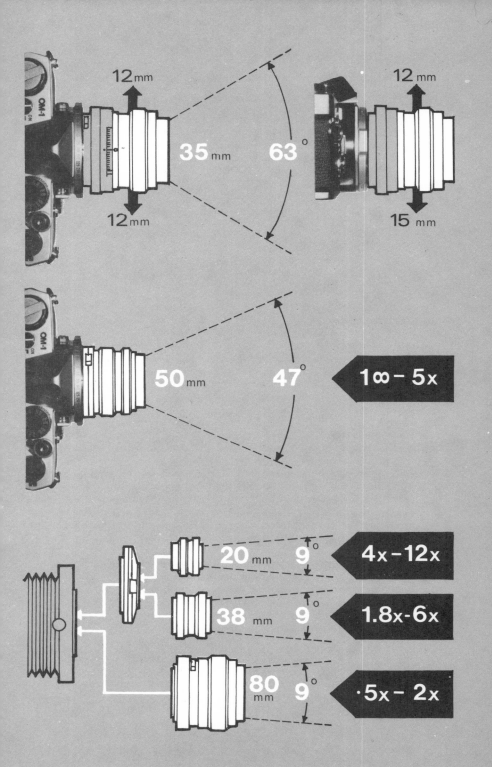

Focusing screens

Changing the screen

To change the screen you need the special tool provided when you buy your alternative screen. You can use your fingers but there is a risk of permanently damaging the screen, mirror or pentaprism with finger marks. Nevertheless, you may find it easier to release the catch by finger pressure rather than pulling on it with the tool.

When the catch is released, the screen and its frame drop down. Grip the protruding tab of the screen with the tool and lift the screen clear. Insert the replacement screen in the same way, grasping the tab with the tool jaws and easing it into position. Push gently upward to secure it.

Interchangeable lenses

A Screen types
- **1** Standard/matt screen with microprism centre
- **2** Microprism/matt type similar to No 1 but for use with the longer telephoto lenses (200 and 300 mm). The standard microprism may darken excessively with such lenses
- **3** Similar to No 1 but with split-image rangefinder. Easier to use when subject has straight lines and for those who have difficulty with microprism focusing
- **4** All matt type for long range and ultra close up work and for those who do not like the obtrusive rangefinder spot
- **5** Clear glass with microprism spot. Very clear image for wide-angle and standard lenses. Cannot be used with the camera's CdS meter
- **6** Similar to No 5 but for standard and telephoto lenses up to 300 mm.
- **7** Similar to Nos 5 and 6 but for lenses of 400 mm and longer
- **8** All-matt screen similar to No 4 specially designed for use with lenses of 300 mm and longer and for photography through astronomical telescopes
- **9** A clear screen designed specifically for endoscopic photography. Cannot be used with the camera's CdS meter
- **10** Matt type with grid patterning for sizing, measuring, lining up subject, etc
- **11** Matt type with central crossed hair lines for critical focusing in close-up and low power macrophotography
- **12** Clear field type with central crossed hair lines for critical focusing in photomicrography and macrophotography at greater than life size
- **13** (not illustrated) A general screen with both microprism and split-image rangefinder in matt field

B   Changing screens
It is advisable to use the special tool provided. Finger marks can cause irreparable damage

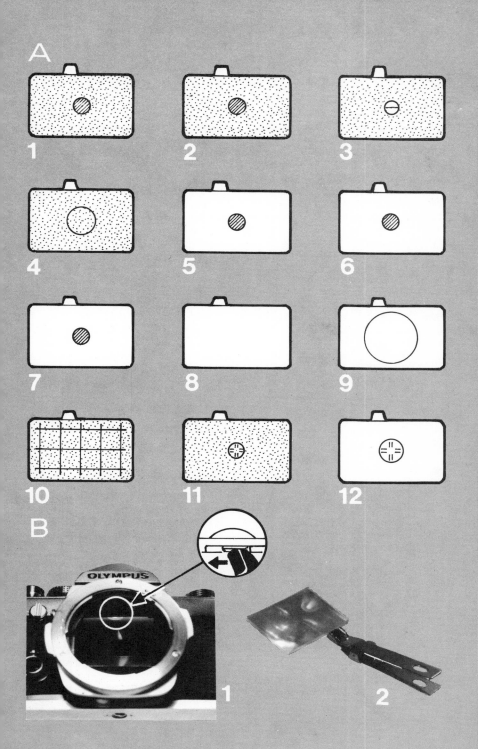

Tele-converter lenses

Telephoto lenses are not inexpensive and if you only occasionally need a rather longer than usual focal length, you might find it rather difficult to justify the expense of acquiring a lens that will be idle for most of the time.

You may, for example, have already purchased a 200 mm lens as a reasonable all-purpose relatively long-distance lens. Perhaps you take photographs at sports meetings or similar events where your viewpoint is necessarily rather distant. The 200 mm lens may be suitable for most of your work, but just occasionally you find that you really need something longer.

An inexpensive solution to the problem and one that saves a lot of space in your gadget bag is a tele-converter – a lens that can be attached to the rear of your camera lens to double or triple its focal length.

How the converter works

Good quality converters are now available. They are simply a group of lenses (at least four elements) that form, in total, a negative unit. When attached to the back of any camera lens, they intercept the converging image-forming rays and lessen their convergence. As a result, the image is spread and brought to a focus farther away from the lens – by a distance equal to the length of the converter. You therefore get a larger image in the film plane. There are models providing 2X enlargements and others 3X. A few give a choice of either, and some are variable between 2X and 3X.

Your 200 mm lens can thus be converted simply and not too expensively into a 400 mm or 600 mm. There are snags, of course. The image quality suffers slightly with the best of converters and if you try to economise still further by buying a bargain-offer converter you are likely to be very disappointed with the results. Also, the image is projected over a greater distance and therefore loses some of its intensity. The loss is more or less in accordance with the inverse square law so your marked apertures are inaccurate. A 200 mm $f4$ lens becomes a 400 mm $f8$ or 600 mm $f12$. But there is a plus: it still focuses down to its normal closest focus.

When to buy

If you need the longer focal length at all regularly, you should not consider the teleconverter unless your economic situation is such that you cannot afford a prime lens. If you need it only very occasionally, however, and you do not intend to enlarge your results excessively – and especially if you can afford to sacrifice a little edge definition, then the tele-converter is worth considering.

Using a tele-converter

With small, timid animals, a close approach is often impossible and shooting from a reasonable distance provides only a small image (1). If you add a tele-converter you may be able to move back a little and still obtain a larger image (2). In these circumstances, even the loss of a little edge definition would not be important.

Olympus Auto Bellows

The Auto Bellows (a deceptive title: it has no auto-diaphragm mechanism except by double cable release) is the basis of the OM-1 and OM-2 macrophotography system. It is designed to take a variety of extra units and provides great versatility in close range work.

Extension range

The extension range of the bellows is 36 mm to 198 mm with the lens in the normal position and 56 mm to 218 mm with the lens panel reversed. To reverse the panel, loosen the screw at the top, loosen the lens shift knob and draw the panel off the rail. Reverse and replace so that the lens is facing the bellows. Slip the bellows over the front of the lens and tighten the screw. This procedure is recommended when shooting at 1:1 or greater with ordinary lenses or the 50 mm f 3.5 Macro lens. It is not necessary with the other macro lenses.

Preparing the bellows for use

Mount the bellows on a tripod, copy stand or other firm support. There are two tripod sockets in the block to allow balancing of various set-ups. Attach the camera body to the bellows before loading it with film. Loosen the clamping screw on the camera mount and remove the mount. Attach it to the camera body as if it were a lens. Reattach mount and camera to bellows and retighten the screw.

Standard lenses, the 80 mm Macro and the 50 mm Macro can be attached to the bellows by lining up the red dots in the normal way and turning clockwise. The 38 mm and 20 mm Macro lenses must first be attached to the Objective Lens Mount PM-MTob.

The auto diaphragm facility of Olympus lenses can be retained only by using a double cable release. The DCR has to be adjusted before loading film into the camera.

The DCR has a lock to enable you to lock the shutter open for long exposures. Depress the plunger and tighten the screw. Loosen the screw to close the shutter.

When using the macro lenses, except the 50 mm you do not need the DCR, because these lenses have no auto diaphragm mechanism.

Metering

Metering with the bellows is carried out in the stop-down mode (see page 40). When fitted to the cameras, the bellows automatically sets the meter for stopped-down operation. To stop an auto lens down for metering, use the depth of field preview lever on the bellows. The OM-2 automatic exposure system works in the usual way.

Olympus Auto Bellows

1	Clamping screw	12	Back rail screw
2	Lens mount panel	13	Bellows
3	Lens mount	14	Connecting ring
4	Depth of field preview	15	Lens shift knob
5	Magnification scale	16	Camera shift knob
6	Extension scale	17	Tripod block
7	Front rail screw	18	Focusing knob
8	Camera body release lever	19	Camera mount clamping screw
9	Camera mounting panel	20	Cable release socket
10	Camera mount	21	Sliding tension adjusters
11	Camera clamping knob	22	Rail clamping knob

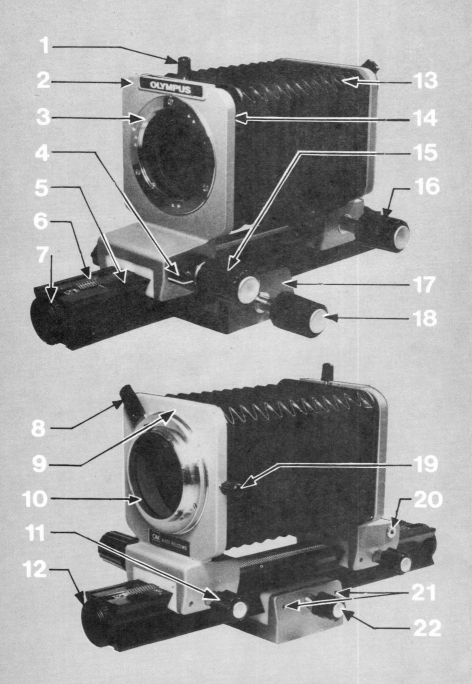

Slide Copier

The Olympus Slide Copier is designed specifically for use with the Olympus Auto Bellows.

Setting up
Mount the camera and lens on the Auto Bellows (see page 72). For 1:1 work it is best to use the 80 mm Macro lens but you can use the 50 mm Macro *f* 3.5 or the 50 mm standard lenses. For copying only part of a slide a shorter focus lens is needed – ideally the 38 mm *f* 3.5 Macro. Set the lens focus ring to infinity, where applicable.

Attach the supporting arm of the slide copier to the tripod block of the bellows with the block tight against the step in the arm. Tighten the arm clamping screw. Line up the bottom of the lens panel with the orange 1X mark on the bellows magnification scale when using the 80 mm lens or with the white 1X or 1.5X, as required, when using 50 mm lenses. Clamp the panel. Use the bellows focusing knob to line up the end of the focusing rail with the same mark on the magnification scale of the slide copier.

Unclamp the bellows on the copier and draw it forward toward the lens. Slip the front of the lens mount inside the clamping ring and tighten the clamping knob.

Insert the slide to be copied in the slot in front of the diffusing glass with the emulsion side toward the camera. Make sure that you push the slide right down. To insert a film strip, pull down the release lever at the bottom of the film holder and slide the film behind the diffusing glass. Adjust the film position and then press the button lock next to the release lever to keep the film holder closed. A roll film stage fits under the film holder by means of two screws.

Focusing
To focus the film or slide to be copied, simply point the complete assembly to any light source and use the bellows focusing knob while looking through the camera viewfinder. Change of image scale is achieved by using the camera shift knob on the bellows and then refocusing.

The film holder can be moved up or down to alter the vertical position of the image. There are red dots on the holder and on the support arm to indicate the normal central position. A film strip can be moved sideways by pushing the button lock and pulling the film in the required direction. The film slot width can also be adjusted by turning the knob below the release lever.

Exposure
Use electronic flash (direct or bounced off a white reflector) or diffused daylight for illumination. With flash work you have to experiment to find the correct distance – except with the Quick Auto 310 on the OM-2 (see page 56) – but with daylight you can use the camera meter as with other bellows work (see page 72).

Slide Copier

1	Slide insertion slot	7	Diffusion glass
2	Roll film stage	8	Roll film stage socket
3	Lens clamp	9	Button lock
4	Lens clamping ring	10	Supporting arm
5	Bellows clip	11	Arm clamping screw
6	Film holder	12	Film slot adjuster

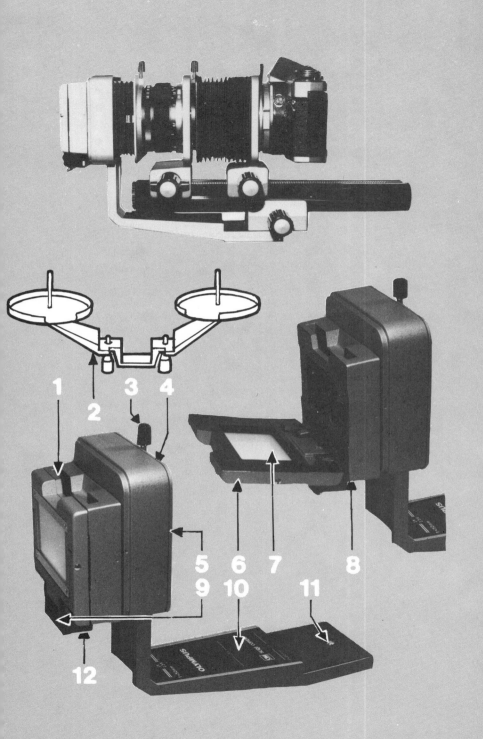

Motor Drive

The Olympus Motor Drive offers powered film transport or sequence shooting with sustained pressure of the firing button. There are arguments for and against sequence shooting particularly when it is used in the hope of catching the decisive moment in an action sequence. It, nevertheless, has advantages when used properly in such applications as motion analysis, security and, in conjunction with other equipment, to make exposures at regular intervals in experimental and scientific work. Motor drives are, however, voracious consumers of film and should be used with caution.

Basic unit

The basic motor drive unit for the OM cameras is extremely small and light in weight. The Motor Drive 1 fixes directly to the tripod socket in the camera base plate. First, you remove the cap on the motor drive socket and store it in a safe place. Offer the motor drive base plate up to the camera base so that the guide pin enters the guide pin hole on the camera base plate. Turn the clamping screw clockwise to secure the unit. To remove the unit, undo the clamping screw, but be sure to replace the socket cap.

When the motor drive is off the camera, the shutter release coupling pin can be moved out of position. If that happens, the unit cannot be attached to the camera. To re-locate the pin, connect the control grip (see page 78) to the motor drive and turn the mode selector to SEQUENCE. Place any small metal object across the camera coupling contacts. The resulting short circuit should restore the pin to its proper place.

OM-1 Motor Drive models

Early models of the Olympus OM-1 were not fitted with motor drive contacts. These models can be identified by the lack of features 2, 4 and 11 (see opposite) on the camera baseplate. They can be fitted with the requisite contacts and baseplate by any Olympus main distributor. OM-1 models that need *no* modification are distinguished by a small MD plate on the front.

Motor drive basic unit

1	Guide pin hole	7	Shutter release coupling pin
2	Film advance claw	8	Guide pin
3	Clamping screw	9	250 Film Back coupling gear
4	Camera coupling contacts	10	Gear cover
5	Terminal contacts	11	Shutter release
6	250 Film Back coupling		

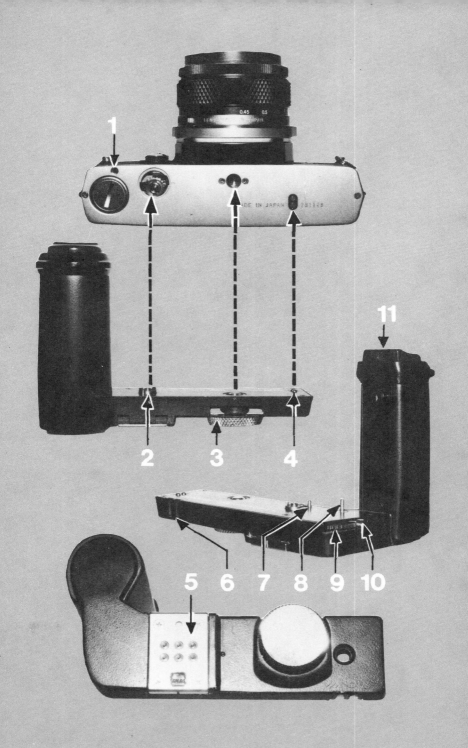

Motor Drive Control Grip

The Olympus motor drive unit is powered by the M18V Control Grip with 1/M18V Battery Holder. The power supply comes from twelve 1.5 volt AA (No 7) dry batteries of the manganese alkaline type (Mallory Mn1500 or equivalent) or twelve 1.25 volt AA (No 7) nickel cadmium (NiCad) rechargeable batteries. The capacity with fresh manganese batteries in normal conditions is about 70 rolls of 36-exposure film.

Loading batteries
Slide the battery holder lock button at the bottom of the grip in the direction of the arrow and the battery holder springs out slightly. Withdraw it completely and insert 12 batteries of the correct type. Be careful to insert the batteries with the correct polarity. The bases go against the springs – the negative contacts – and the small top contacts against the metal contacts in the holder – the positive contacts. Push the battery holder back into the grip until it locks into place.

To remove the batteries, press them from the positive end to compress the springs and lever them out. You should always remove the batteries from the holder if you do not expect to use the unit in the next few weeks – particularly if the batteries have been well used.

Attaching the control grip
To attach the control grip to the motor drive unit, line up the index line on the rear of the grip with the line on the rear frame of the motor drive to engage the catch at the back of the grip just above the mode selector. Push the grip forward and up until it snaps into the mount on the front of the motor drive.

Operating sequence
Move the shutter release lock lever on the control grip forward and up. Turn the mode selector to SINGLE or SEQUENCE as required. Release the shutter by pressing either the release on the control grip or the top of the motor drive. With single shooting the camera then makes one exposure and the motor winds the film on ready for the next pressure on the release. With sequence shooting, the shutter release remains in action as long as you keep your finger on it. But watch it! In ideal conditions it can shoot five frames a second.

You can use all shutter speeds for single frame shooting and all except the one second speed on sequence shooting.

Turn the mode selector to OFF when not shooting and lock the release on the control grip. The release on the motor drive has no lock.

To remove the control grip, turn the mode selector to OFF and lock the shutter release. Push the grip detach button on the top front of the grip and lift the grip off.

Motor drive control grip

1	Non-slip grip	6	Grip locks
2	Shutter release	7	Mode selector
3	Grip detach button	8	Battery holder lock
4	Electrical contacts	9	Battery holder
5	Shutter release lock		

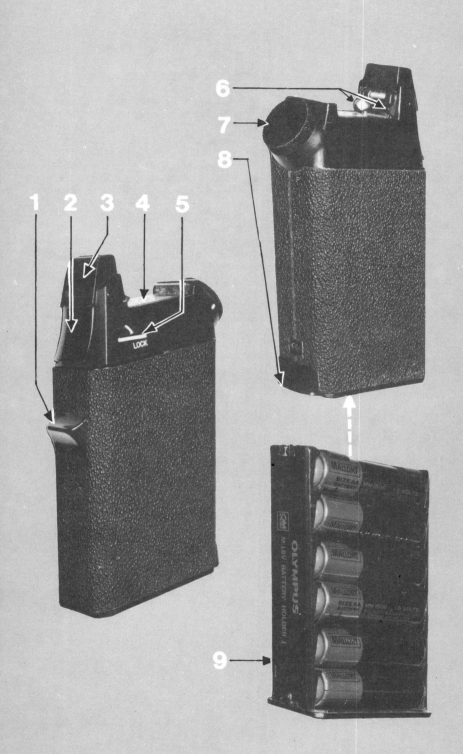

250 Film Back

The normal camera back can be completely removed from the OM cameras by opening it (see page 32) and pressing down on the exposed part of the pin hinge.

To mount the 250 Back, turn the large knobs on top of the magazine chambers (the open/close knobs) to OPEN. Turn the small knob marked "clamp" under the left hand magazine chamber (viewed from the front) as far as it will go against the direction of the arrow. Place the rewind end of the camera on to the camera stage at the right hand end of the 250 Back, then lower the other end into position. Hold the camera tight against the film back and turn the clamp knob in the direction of the arrow to bring the camera clamp plate on to the front of the camera.

Attach the motor drive to the camera – if you have not already done so. Either method can be used.

Loading the magazines
Dismantle one magazine (they are identical) by pressing the domed button on the top and turning the serrated rim clockwise until the openings in both parts coincide. The inner shield and spool can then be removed. In total darkness, cut a taper on the end of your roll of film and insert it into the slot of the spool, emulsion down. Do not fold or otherwise secure the film end. Spool any length of film up to 10 m and place the spool in the outer shield leaving about 10 cm (4 in) protruding in the direction of the wind. Replace the inner shield by lining up the openings and dropping it in. Hold the protruding film securely against the magazine and turn the inner shield clockwise with the flat button on the top. It locks into place with a click. Repeat the operation in room lighting with the other end of the film and the other magazine but fold the tip of the film back to form a hook of about 6 mm ($\frac{1}{4}$ in) to catch in the slot.

Loading the back
Turn the open/close knobs to OPEN and lift the rear cover lock. Remove the back cover by sliding it slightly to the left and lifting clear. Pull down the fork knobs on the bottom of each chamber.

Place the magazines in the chambers – the full one at the rewind end – lining up the red index marks on the magazines with the white index marks on each chamber. Push back the fork knobs and turn the one on the rewind (feed) end clockwise gently to take up any slack in the film. Hook the left end of the rear cover on to the back and press the other end to lock. Turn the open/close knobs to CLOSE. Make five blind exposures and check that the fork knob on the feed chamber rotates. Set exposure counter and film reminder.

To unload, when the counter indicates O, turn it back to 10, cover the camera lens and advance the film six frames to wind off the last few exposed frames. Turn the open/close knobs to OPEN, remove back, pull down fork knobs and invert the back to extract the magazines.

250 Film Back

1	Rear cover	8	Film reminder	14	Camera clamp
2	Lock	9	Inner shield	15	Pressure plate
3	Open/close knob	10	Spool	16	Motor drive coupling
4	Take-up chamber	11	Fork knob		terminal
5	Outer shield	12	Clamp knob	17	Fork knob
6	Feed chamber	13	Motor drive		
7	Open/close knob		coupling gear		

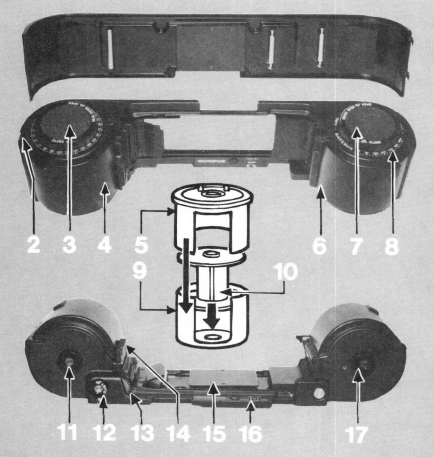

Motor drive combinations

There are four basic motor drive combinations for the Olympus OM cameras. Basic combination A has been described in the previous pages. It consists of the motor drive unit fitted directly to the camera base and the M18V control grip fitted to the motor drive.

Combination B uses the Relay Cord 1.2 m to allow a 1.2 metre extension between the motor drive and the control grip. The photographer can thus carry the control grip in his pocket to keep it warm and dry in adverse weather conditions or simply to reduce the weight in his hand. There is also a 10 m relay cord.

Combination C allows for the fact that the motor drive can (with fresh top-quality batteries, free-running cassettes and in reasonably warm weather) dispose of 36 frames in 7 or 8 seconds. The 250 Film Back gives you up to 10 m of film in one load. The complete combination C weighs about 2 kg which, although no mean weight, is remarkably light for the facilities it provides.

Combination D brings the AC Control Box into use instead of the battery-loaded control grip. The motor drive can then be run from household current. The control box has its own sequence timer to allow framing rates from 4 per second to one frame every 120 seconds. It is connected to the motor drive by Relay Cord 1.2 m or 10 m.

Ancillary equipment

The 1.2 m Relay Cord serves the normal function described above but also provides a terminal for radio or cable remote control and another for the connection of external DC power sources.

The 10 m Relay Cord provides remote control of the motor drive from a useful distance but it induces a voltage drop if used with battery power. It is best used in conjunction with the AC Control Box.

The AC Control Box can power two motor drives. It has a single frame facility and the built in timer described above.

The 250 Film Back is described on page 80. A film loader is available for rapid loading of the film magazines from 33 m (100 ft) rolls. It has a counter mechanism to stop loading at preset lengths.

Motor drive combinations

A Basic combination of Motor Drive and Control Grip.
B Motor Drive, Control Grip and Relay Cord to allow the grip to be detached from the motor drive.
C Motor Drive, Control Grip and 250 Film Back.
D Motor Drive, Relay Cord and AC Control Box.

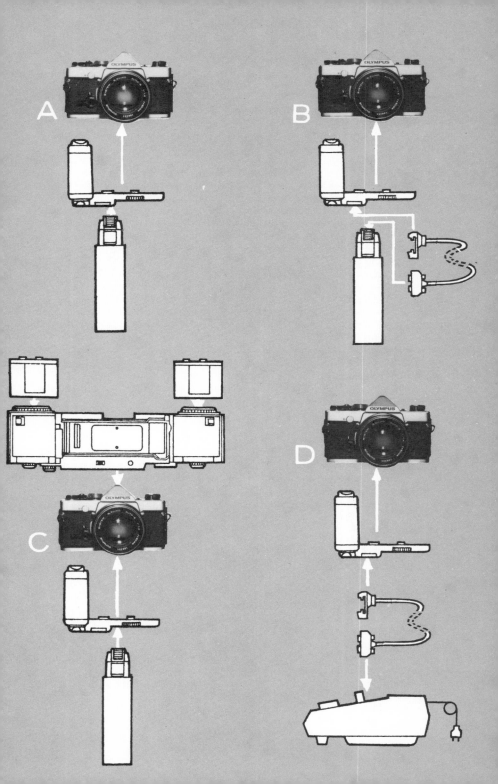

Close-up equipment

Although the standard lenses for the OM cameras can focus to 45 cm ($17\frac{3}{4}$ in) you may need to get closer than that on occasions. The range of close-up equipment available includes close-up attachment lenses, extension tubes and the 50 mm macro lens. Ancillary equipment includes the Varimagni Finder, Eyecup and interchangeable focusing screens.

Close-up lenses

The simplest way to adapt your camera, fitted with a standard lens, to close-range work is to attach close-up lenses, sometimes called supplementary lenses, to the front of the camera lens. The principle of a close-up lens (available from various manufacturers) is explained on page 123. Olympus supply lenses said to be of 40 cm focal length and focusing from 45 to 19 cm, using the focusing travel of the camera lens. There are two versions, for 49 mm or 55 mm filter threads.

Extension tubes

Supplementary lenses are generally single-glass lenses and the image quality obtainable from them is restricted. A preferable method for close focusing is to use extension tubes to increase the distance between the lens and the film. The extension tubes made for the OM cameras are 7, 14 and 25 mm in length. They can be used singly or together to focus at much closer range than is generally possible with close-up lenses. When all three are placed behind a 50 mm lens for example they allow a reproduction ratio approaching 1:1.

These tubes do not operate the Olympus auto-diaphragm mechanism or allow full aperture metering to be used. When attached to the camera they convert it to stopped-down operation (see page 40).

Focusing aids

The Varimagni Finder can be attached to the viewfinder eyepiece to allow viewing at any angle. It also serves for critical focusing by providing a choice of 1.2X magnification of the whole image area or 2.5X enlargement of the central portion.

The Eyecup is a useful item when you do not use the Varimagni. It attaches to the viewfinder eyepiece and provides a soft rubber shield both for the eye or spectacles and to prevent light reaching the meter sensors and so influencing meter readings. It also takes eyesight correction lenses, available in strengths from plus 2 to minus 5 dioptres.

Close-up equipment

A Eyecup for viewfinder eyepiece. Can be fitted with eyesight correction lenses

B Interchangeable screens allow a choice of screen for close range work

C Varimagni Finder, for convenient viewing and critical focusing

D Extension tubes to increase lens-to-film distance

E Standard lenses, particularly suited for use with close-up equipment: 1, 55 mm f 1.2. 2, 50 mm f 1.8, 3, 50 mm f 1.4, 4, 50 mm f 3.5 macro.

F Close-up lenses: 1, 55 mm fitting for 55 mm f 1.2 lens. 2, 49 mm fitting for other standard lenses, including 50 mm f 3.5 macro

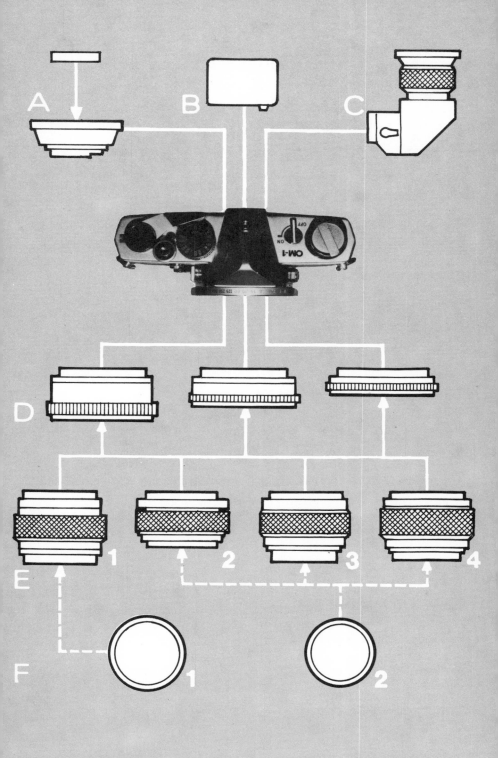

Macrophotography equipment

Close-up photography is impressive enough, but macrophotography enables us to photograph detail that is invisible to the human eye. Exactly where close-up photography ends and macrophotography begins is open to argument but the macro equipment available for the Olympus OM cameras certainly takes us well into the macro field by any definition.

The basis for extreme close range work is the Auto Bellows, described on page 72. It can be used on a tripod in conjunction with the camera and any lens but the most suitable lenses are those of standard focal length and the special macro lenses (see page 66). The shorter the focal length, the greater the magnification. The 20 mm macro lens for example can provide a magnification of 12:1 with the bellows, while the 50 mm standard and macro lenses can go only to 4:1.

Useful accessories for close range work with or without the bellows are the focusing stage and focusing rail. The rail is primarily designed for mounting on a tripod, copy stand, etc to allow back and forth motions of the camera without moving the support. It has the additional feature of allowing side to side movement. The stage is an intermediate piece between camera and rail.

For really ambitious macro work, Olympus market their Macrophotographic Equipment PMT-35, which can be adapted to the OM cameras. It consists of epi-illuminators, filters, stage plates and adaptors, interchangeable supporting arm, the three macro lenses, a substage transmitter-light illuminator and even a spare bulb — all as accessories, of course, to the basic ·unit.

Macrophoto equipment

A Auto Bellows and accessories. 1, Auto Bellows. 2, Double cable release. 3, Interchangeable screens. 4, Varimagni Finder. 5, Eyecup and correction lens.
B Focusing Rail and Stage: 1, Focusing stage. 2, Focusing rail.
C Macrophoto Equipment PMT-35; 1, OM-mount adaptor. 2, Stage.

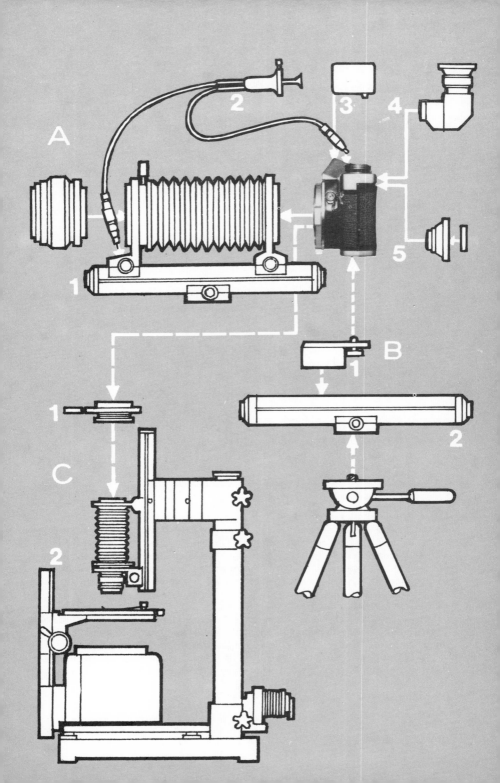

Olympus filters

Filters alter the light (or other radiation) reaching the film. Olympus produce a series of filters for use with their lenses.

For colour transparency films
Coloured filters used with reversal films alter the colour of the final transparency, either for effect or to correct a tendency toward "incorrect" colour.

Effect of filter on colour slides

Filter	Colour	Effect
Ultra-violet	UV absorbing	Haze cutting. Reduces blue cast near water, snow etc.
Skylight	Very pale pink	Similar to UV filter, but also makes pictures slightly warmer.
Neutral density	Grey	Reduces light without altering the colour, for exposure control.
Polarizing	Grey	Allows through only light polarized in one plane, for reducing reflections or darkening skies.
Blue	Light blue	For use with low, red, sunlight.
	Mid blue	For using daylight type film with clear flashbulbs (*not* electronic)
	Deep blue	For using daylight film with studio floods.
Amber	Light amber	For use with daylight film in dull bluish lighting outdoors.
	Deep amber	For using type A (tungsten) film in daylight.

For colour negative films
Colour negative films do not need accurate filtration in the camera because the colour balance can be corrected in printing. A polarizing filter acts exactly as it does with transparency films, and UV absorbing filters may afford some degree of haze penetration. Optimum colour can be attained with professional type colour films only if they are approximately balanced to the light source.

For black-and-white films
Polarizing and neutral density filters have the same effect as they do with colour films, and ultra-violet absorbing filters may reduce haze. Coloured filters, however, simply alter the relative tones of different coloured parts of the subject.

The Olympus range includes Yellow (Y48), Orange (O56) and Red (R60) filters. They are all high-quality optical glass types and are coated on both sides.

Olympus filters

The Olympus range of filters for colour and black and white films.

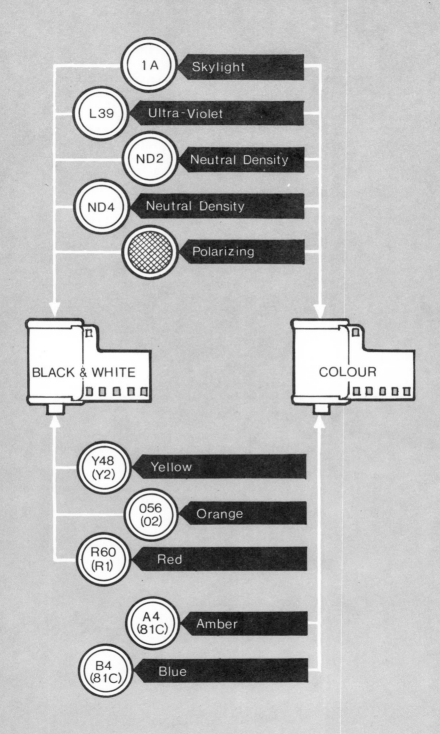

Camera supports

When it is convenient to do so, it is always advisable to mount the camera on a tripod or other firm support. Most people overestimate their ability to hold a camera still at the moment of exposure and many never realise that their pictures could be a great deal sharper than they are.

There are many models of tripod and not a few of them are far too flimsy to be of any use with a comparatively lightweight 35 mm camera. Choose the sturdiest you can afford, with firmly locking legs and a positive lock on the centre column, if provided, and the pan/tilt or ball and socket-head.

Miniature tripod

The smaller stand (C) is useful in many situations where a full size tripod cannot be accommodated. It can rest on a table, chair, wall, car roof, etc. and provide adequate support for long exposures. Similar small supports with clamps (B), spikes and other methods of securing them are supplied by various manufacturers and can be of great value where longer exposures are necessary.

Another type of support that sometimes helps to hold long lenses steady is the pistol grip (E), although its greatest value is probably in conjunction with a support for the left hand so that the barrel of the lens can be laid across the left elbow. The pistol grip usually has a built in cable release to allow the shutter to be fired from its trigger.

Cable release

This is a plunger type release which screws into the shutter button for tripod mounted shots, because finger pressure on the shutter release could quite easily set up vibrations in the tripod. For long time exposures with the shutter speed dial at B a cable release with a lock-down facility is valuable. You need not then hold onto the release throughout the exposure.

The mounting on top of the tripod takes many forms, too, but the most popular are the ball and socket (D), allowing the camera to be tilted in almost any direction, and the pan-and-tilt (A), which allows only an up and down tilt or a 360-degree horizontal swivel. The pan-and-tilt usually has a larger mounting platform for the camera and more positive locking.

Tripods and other supports

A Pan/tilt head	**D** Ball and socket
B Clamp and table stand	**E** Pistol grip with
C Miniature tripod	cable release

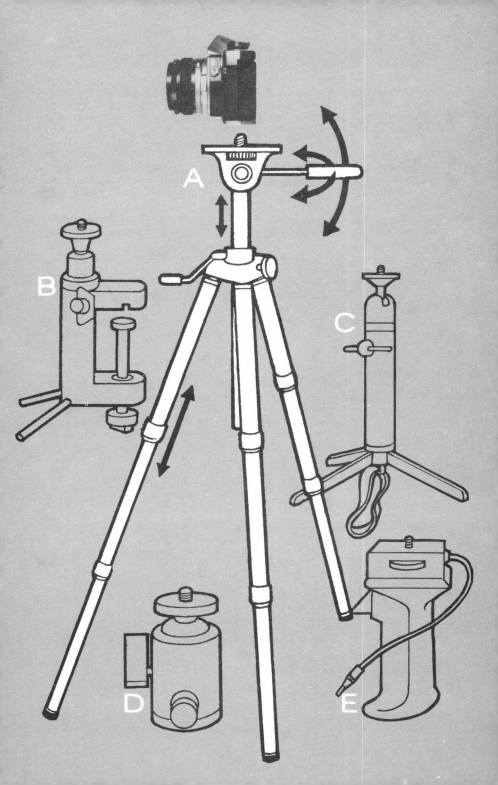

Copying equipment

Somewhere in between ordinary close-range work and high magnification macro work comes the type of photography often referred to as copying. Olympus offer various items of equipment in this field for those who do not aspire to or, indeed, cannot afford their full macrophotographic equipment.

Portable copy stand
The simplest item is the Pen Up 3 portable copy stand with four telescopic legs designed to set the boundaries of the area covered and the focused distance with camera and standard lens. Naturally, this is not so important with a reflex camera and focusing can be carried out normally for any size of subject that can be framed. Originally designed to take lenses with 45 mm filter threads, the Pen Up 3 is supplied with an adaptor to allow the standard 50 mm and 50 mm Macro lenses to be attached.

Macrophoto Stand VST-1
A more specialised item is the Macrophoto Stand VST-1, designed for photographing items about the size of a postage stamp. An adapter can be clamped to the post to support the bellows or focusing rail. The stand is supplied with a round frosted stage plate (black on the reverse) for incident light and many other stage plates are available. An extension bar can be attached to the post to increase lens-to-subject distance.

Standard copy stand
Naturally, Olympus supply an orthodox copy stand of the baseboard and column variety. The column is of sturdy H-section construction and provides facilities for connecting a twin-light unit to the top front edge. The lamps are on flexible arms that can be adjusted to a variety of positions. Anti-vibration clamps bearing on the top and edge of the baseboard are also available. A tripod screw attachment on the robust supporting arm allows you to attach the camera alone or via the focusing stage with or without the focusing rail, or the Auto Bellows.

Copying equipment

A Pen Up 3 portable copying stand
B Macrophoto Stand VST-1
C Copy Stand

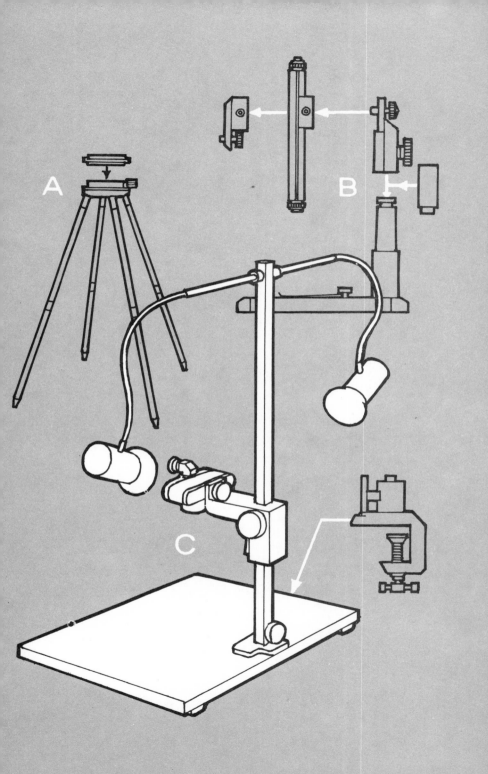

Colour films

There are two types of colour film in common use—negative and reversal. Negative films are processed to produce images which are reversed in both colour and tone from the original subject. These are then used to produce colour prints. Reversal films are processed to produce a positive image closely resembling the original subject. The image is viewed either by transmitted light or projected on to a screen.

How they work

When a colour film is exposed, it produces a latent image in the same way as a black-and-white film. During processing, this is converted to a coloured dye image, the dyes being formed together with silver grains. The silver is then removed to leave the coloured dyes. In a colour negative film, the dyes correspond to the silver formed from the original latent image. They are designed also to be of complementary (opposite) colours to the original subject. In a reversal film, the original latent image is developed, and the film then re-exposed to light. On re-development, coloured dyes are produced only when (and where) the second image develops.

Exposure latitude

Just like black-and-white films, colour films must be given the right exposure. This is particularly important for reversal films, because there is no intermediate printing stage. The density of the final transparency is determined by the exposure in the

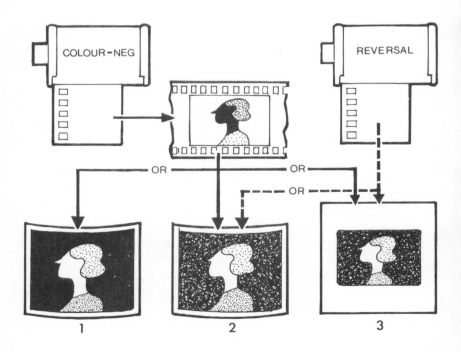

Colour negative film is for colour prints (2) *but colour slides* (3) *or black-and-white prints* (1) *can be made. Colour reversal film is for slides but can be used for prints, too.*

camera, which for optimum results should be correct to within half a stop. Colour negative films can produce adequate colour representation if over exposed up to two stops, or underexposed one stop. Film manufacturers supply meter settings (ASA and DIN ratings) for colour films. These will give normal results but, like any other exposure recommendation, should be modified to suit your equipment and viewing preferences.

Colour of lighting

Lighting varies greatly in colour, from the almost red light of an open fire to the strong blue of a blue sky (without sunlight). Normal daylight is a mixture of blue skylight and yellow sunlight. Our eyes adapt to the colour of lighting, but colour films do not. Compensation can be made when printing from colour negatives, but transparency films must be balanced for the light source in use. Manufacturers produce different types: Daylight—for use in daylight and with electronic flash or blue flashbulbs; Tungsten, Type A—for photolamps (3400 K) and Type B for use with studio lamps or tungsten halogen lamps (3200 K). A white object lit by a 60 watt bulb and and pictured on a daylight type film comes out a bright orange colour; whereas lit by daylight it comes out blue on a tungsten light film. Filters are available to provide correct colour balance when using a film in lighting other than that for which it is balanced.

Film speeds and image qualities

As their speed rises, colour films increase in graininess, while decreasing in contrast and colour saturation. The change in graininess and contrast being more marked than it is on black-and-white films for the same change in film speeds. Because the grain is multi-coloured, it may be considered more objectionable than that on black-and-white photographs. All commonly available colour negative films are of moderate speed (64–100 ASA, 19–21 DIN), and give results comparable with medium speed black-and-white films. Transparency films are available in slow (20–32 ASA, 14–16 DIN), moderate (64–100 ASA, 19–21 DIN) and fast (160–200 ASA, 23–24 DIN). Faster films and special processing should be reserved for cases of necessity. Many photographers use the slowest possible transparency films to give them the greatest colour saturation and sharpest images. This is particularly important if any of the pictures are to be offered for reproduction. The fast films have a distinguishable grain, but this is not noticeable at normal projection distances.

Choice of film type

Apart from the choice of (reversal) film speed, one must choose between reversal and negative films for any particular use.

Colour transparencies are ideal for group viewing, and projected images are more closely comparable to the original than are prints. They are also suitable for use as originals for photomechanical reproduction. The finest colour prints can be made from transparencies, but they are extremely expensive. Conventional colour prints made from transparencies, however, are not usually as good as those made from colour negatives.

Colour negatives can be printed directly to give either prints or transparencies of equal quality. Negative films are thus the first choice for making prints or when the final form is undecided. The main disadvantage of negative films is the cost of printing. This can be significantly reduced, however, by making (or having made) only those prints you want to keep. A number of laboratories will process a film and return it with a contact sheet so that you can select the negatives before any prints are made.

The colour pictures

There are few subjects that you cannot shoot satisfactorily with an Olympus OM camera. They are single-lens reflexes, which means that the viewing image is large and bright, making framing and focusing easy. It also means that you can use a variety of lenses and attachments on the camera.

People

People always make popular subjects, mainly because they can be presented in so many different ways. They can be playing, working, running, jumping, thinking, talking or looking glamorous. Commonly, they are pictured doing nothing in particular and the main object then is to present a reasonable likeness. Even that presentation takes various forms. You can have a formal portrait, a snapshot taken without the subject's knowledge (we used to call that candid photography) or something in between, like the child study opposite. This type of shot is best taken with a slightly longer-focus lens (say 90–135 mm) to get a large image without distortion of the features caused by going too close. You have to watch the lighting outdoors, too. It can be contrasty, while a semi-diffused lighting is generally much better for portraiture. Colour casts can also be a problem if your subject is close to reflective matter, such as grass, foliage, coloured walls, etc.

Action

Photographing people in action calls for a variety of techniques and one of the most interesting is that of panning the camera. This simply means that, instead of holding the camera still to keep the image of a stationary or slow-moving subject in the same place on the film, you achieve the same object by moving the camera to follow a fast-moving subject. You can follow only the general line of direction, however. The long-jumper's body, for example, is reasonably sharp, but his arms and legs, moving erratically, are blurred.

Choose your picture

When you first see an interesting subject, your immediate reaction may be to photograph it complete—as an object in itself. Frequently, however, the part is more interesting than the whole. The townsman might find a harvester unusual and therefore interesting. The agricultural worker might not. But both might be able to appreciate the pattern of lines and curves formed by wheels and belts. The nature of the real subject is immaterial in such a picture. It has been created by concentrating on a detail instead of the whole scene.

Natural beauty

Out and about, whether in town or country, pictures are very much what you make of them. They reflect, to a large extent, your personal interests. The scene appeals to you, so you photograph it. Unfortunately, the resulting picture so often bears no resemblance to your appreciation of the original. The cause is usually a lack of awareness on your part, often because you forgot to concentrate the interest. A single tree, shot from a carefully chosen viewpoint, can evoke the atmosphere of a scene in a way that an overall shot possibly cannot.

Go in close

Similarly, a garden full of flowers may present a pleasing picture to the ranging eye but contain too much for the fixed stare of the camera. When you pick out on a single bloom, or a cluster, or a pattern, using close-up equipment if necessary, the interest is concentrated and easier to take in.

Photographs by: Peter Styles (pages 97, 100–101, 103); Colour Library International (page 98); P. C. Poynter (page 99); Colin Ramsey (page 102); Raymond Lea (page 104).

Animals

Animals run people a close second in the popular subject stakes and horses have a place of their own in most people's affections. Many people profess to dislike animals but few extend that dislike to the horse. They may be a little nervous of its size but they rarely actively dislike it.

It is not easy to photograph horses in a group. You may need a lot of patience while you wait for them to move into close proximity and a reasonably satisfying composition. You need to choose location and viewpoint with some care, too, because distracting background objects or distorted perspective do not help at all. The horse is a large animal, with quite a distance between his ears and his tail. If you approach too closely, one end will look a great deal larger than the other. You have to stand well back and shoot with a longer focus lens.

Glamour

Glamour photography (a loose overall description for a subject that has innumerable variations) would be much more popular if it were not so difficult. It tends to be the field of a relatively few specialists. Its success depends so much on the ability (and suitability) of the model and on the photographer's single-minded concentration on the required results. The model is the total subject. Backgrounds and props should usually be kept to the absolute minimum so that they attract virtually no attention at all.

Colour principles

Shooting in colour is not significantly different from shooting in black and white. It is, in fact, possible for the newcomer in colour, already familiar with black and white photography, to become hypnotised by colour to such an extent that he forgets that his main aim is to produce a picture. He tends to introduce coloured objects into his picture or to search out colourful scenes. Those who start their photography in colour are not usually afflicted in this way.

Mood and perspective

Nevertheless, there are a few principles that it is as well to recognise. Colours do tend to have certain effects connected with mood and perspective. Colours in the reddish half of the spectrum gives an impression of warmth, gaiety, garishness, danger, etc. according to the type of picture. The bluer colours are cooler, more sober, sometimes even depressing. Saturated colours are brash, brilliant, harsh, etc. whereas desaturated, pastel colours are delicate, soothing and soft. The bluer colours are less insistent and tend to sink into the background, while the redder colours tend to thrust forward and to attract the eye.

Colour harmony

We hear a lot about colour harmony, too, but this is a difficult subject on which to pontificate in photography. Where the picture is intended to be restful and soothing, it is a good general principle to include only colours that harmonise. But colour contrast and even clash is probably just as important. A certain amount of contrast is necessary in most pictures but the contrasting colour should generally be a relatively small part of the total scene—like the accessories in a lady's outfit.

In most pictures you accept the colours as they are but where any degree of contrivance is present or when you have reasonable control over the picture content there are a few points worth watching. Just as in black and white you should look for the obtrusive detail that has no relevance to the picture but in colour, you should pay particular attention where possible to red or other bright-coloured objects in the background. An outdoor portrait for example might be perfectly acceptable in black and white if a telephone kiosk or pillar box appeared out of focus in a small part of the background. In colour, such a defocused red blob would be distracting.

Similarly, any fussy background can generally be obscured in black and white by differential focusing. Colour backgrounds may still obtrude even when defocused.

Colour casts

Colour casts can be a problem. The black and white worker might be totally unprepared for the bluish features that can be produced by a wide-brimmed blue hat, the green reflected on to a white dress by grass or nearby foliage, or even the bright blue that can be reflected by snow from a brilliant blue sky.

An equally ineradicable cast can be produced by mixing light sources. There are colour films for use in daylight, others for use in artificial light and colour print films that are generally suitable for either type of lighting. No colour film, however, can render all colours accurately when exposed to both daylight or its equivalents and artificial light. The result is an orange-red cast in the parts of a daylight film affected by artificial light and a bluish cast in the parts of an artificial light film affected by daylight. Thus, if you use fill-in lighting you must use electronic flash, blue flash-bulbs or neutral coloured (preferably white) reflectors with daylight film and tungsten lighting or neutral-coloured reflectors with artificial light film. With colour print film, all your lighting must be of the same type or colour temperature.

Colour temperature

Films may be exposed to any light source, and—provided that they receive the correct exposure—will produce an image. Whatever the source, black-and-white films normally produce a satisfactory picture, but colour films require more carefully selected sources. The most important quality of a light source for colour photography is its colour. Everyday light varies from strong orange produced by household tungsten lamps to the pronounced blue of a clear blue sky—such as illuminates subjects in the shadow on a sunny day. Our eyes can compensate for different colours of overall lighting: we see white objects as white with any normal light source. Colour films, however, cannot compensate, and the colour balance of pictures is influenced by the colour of the light source.

The colour quality of light may be defined as its colour temperature. This is achieved by referring to the colour of light radiated by a theoretically perfect radiator heated to any particular temperature, which is measured in kelvins (K). Thus a light source radiating light of the same quality as the radiator at 5000 K is said to have a colour temperature of 5000 K. Low colour temperature (e.g. 2500 K) indicates a yellow or orange colour, and high colour temperature (e.g. 10000 K) a blue colour.

Colour films

Colour films are balanced for particular light sources. Unless they are used with the right source, or the correct filter is used, they will not give a normal colour balance. For most purposes this is important only with reversal films—the colour balance of negatives can be corrected at the printing stage. Three types of reversal film are in common use: Daylight; type A, for use with 3400 K photolamps (over-run lamps such as Photofloods); and type B for use with 3200 K studio lamps or tungsten halogen lamps. Daylight type film is suitable for use with electronic flash (although a pale yellow filter is desirable with some units) and with blue coated flashbulbs.

Colour temperatures of some light sources

Light source	Colour temperature (K)
Skylight	12000–18000
Overcast sky	8000
Photographic 'white flame' carbon arc	7400
World average daylight	6500
Sunlight (noon)	5400
Daylight (sky and sun)	5500
English standard daylight	4800
Electronic flash	5500–7000
Blue coated flashbulb	5300
Flashcube and Magicube	4950
Low temperature carbon arc	4000
Clear flashbulb (aluminium filled)	3800
Photolamp 3400 K	3400
Tungsten studio lamp	3200
*Tungsten halogen lamp	3200
1000 watt & 500 watt floods	3000
General service bulb 200 watt	3000
General service bulb 100 watt	2900

* Photographic Studio type—others are variable

Fluorescent light sources do not always produce a continuous spectrum (i.e. light of all colours may not be equally represented), and give unpredictable results with colour films. After careful tests specially made "colour matching" tubes may prove satisfactory, but normal general service tubes are unlikely to give good pictures. When their use is unavoidable, a rough guide is to use daylight film and a red filter of the type designed for colour printing (about a 40R) with cold white tubes, and to use type B film (no filter) with warm white tubes.

The only way of ensuring accurate colour pictures when using an unknown combination of film and light source is to make a series of test exposures. For such a purpose you need a complete set of pale coloured filters—which must be of optical quality. Such filters are usually of real value only to the professional photographer.

Do not, however, be overcautious in matching even transparency films to light sources. For example, although you should use a pale blue filter, you can get quite acceptable results using unfiltered type B films with household lamps. In fact, some people prefer the warmer flesh-tones produced by this technique to correct colours. Slight over-exposure tends to minimize colour imbalance by lightening the overall density.

Mixed light sources

One very important factor, if you are to obtain an even colour balance overall, is to ensure that all the lighting used in one picture is the same colour temperature. This is just as important for colour negative films as it is for transparency films, because the colour balance of one part of a picture cannot be altered without altering the rest. The normal rule of thumb is that light sources should not differ in colour temperature by more than 100 K. Studio photographers use large pieces of filter in front of lights if they want to alter colour temperature. This is beyond most other photographers, but the use of small filters over electronic flash tubes can solve some problems. For example, using type A film an electronic flash could be mixed with photolamp (3400 K) illumination if the requisite (type A film used in daylight) filter were fitted over the flash head.

Black-and-white films

The vast majority of black-and-white films are processed to produce negatives. They consist of an emulsion of silver halides in gelatin, coated on a transparent flexible base. When this is exposed correctly, it forms an invisible *latent* image. During development the visible image of silver particles forms. The silver is deposited in proportion to the light which was focused on the film from the subject. Thus the negative is dark where the subject was light, and vice versa. When a print is made from a negative, silver is deposited in the print emulsion in proportion to the light passing through the negative and thus depicts the tones of the original subject. The characteristics of a negative depend on the type of film used, and on the processing it is given.

Grain
When a negative is magnified, it is possible to see the clumps of silver grains that form the image. This is called the grain or graininess of the negative and is proportional to the film speed; that is, the faster a film, the greater will be its grain. The grain is also influenced by the exposure and processing used. Any deviation from the normal recommendations for the film and developer—especially over-exposing or over-developing—is likely to lead to increased grain.

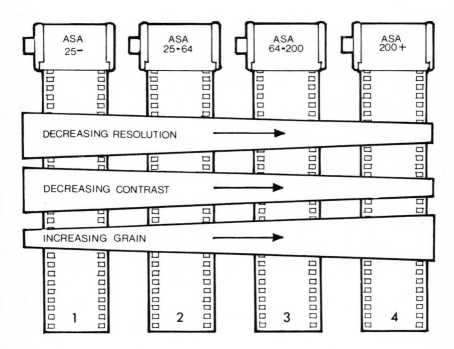

Generally speaking, films of low sensitivity to light are formed from smaller and more evenly spaced silver halide grains. Thus, the slower the film, the less noticeable the granular structure on enlargement and the higher the resolution. Common uses are: 1, very slow films, fine copying work. 2, slow films, static or brilliantly lit subjects. 3, medium speed, average photography. 4, fast, low-light photography.

Contrast

The range of grey tones a film can produce between black and white is called its contrast. Extremely high contrast materials record most of a subject as either black or white, whereas low contrast materials can give a wide range of greys between the two extremes. Normal camera films all have an acceptable contrast for general pictorial use, although the more contrasty ones give less highlight and shadow detail in pictures of high contrast subjects. As a rule, the faster a film, the lower its contrast. Prolonging the processing increases the contrast at the expense of increasing the grain.

Colour sensitivity

Untreated silver halides are sensitive only to blue light (and ultraviolet radiation). Modern photographic emulsions incorporate dyes which make them sensitive to other colours. General-purpose camera films have a sensitivity roughly the same as the human eye—and are designated *panchromatic*. High speed films have an extended red sensitivity, and some specialised emulsions are sensitive either only to blue, or to blue and green. The latter are called *orthochromatic*. The reaction of a film to different colours can be altered by the use of filters.

Exposure latitude

The best negatives are produced when the film is given the optimum exposure. However, errors of up to one stop make little difference, and printable negatives can be produced with exposures up to three stops away from the ideal, but such negatives are more difficult to print. They also have little shadow detail, if they are underexposed, or little highlight detail if they are overexposed— nor do they give as good enlargements as correctly exposed negatives. Deviation from normal processing recommendations may alter the effective speed, and special processing may be used to "retrieve" drastically mis-exposed films. It does not, however, give excellent results.

Other characteristics

Film manufacturers refer to the *acutance* or edge sharpness and *resolving power* of their films. These are two characteristics which affect the sharpness of a photographic image, but all modern films produce so sharp an image that they are characteristics of interest only in specialist applications. All modern general-purpose films also carry an anti-halation backing to prevent light that has passed through the emulsion being reflected back and degrading the image.

Choice of film

The contrast and graininess of a negative determine the degree to which the image can be enlarged. For most purposes a medium speed film (80–160 ASA, 20–23 DIN) will prove ideal. Carefully processed 35 mm negatives can yield virtually grain-free prints up to 15 × 12 inches. Slow films (20–40 ASA, 11–14 DIN) are best if you need big enlargements, and fast films 400–500 ASA, 27–28 DIN) are needed for dull conditions or fast action photography. Films faster than this (or special processing for extra speed) usually give unacceptably grainy images, and should be avoided except when there is no alternative.

Loading film cassettes

One of the advantages of 35 mm photography is the comparative cheapness of the film used. The standard cassette can take a full load of 36 pictures, which would need three rolls of 120 size film for $2\frac{1}{4} \times 2\frac{1}{4}$ inch pictures at about 50% greater cost.

The advantage is even greater if you load your own cassettes. A cassette refill of 36 exposures costs only about 60% of the loaded cassette price. But you can also obtain 5 m of 35 mm film to provide three cassette reloads at even lower cost or 17 m to provide 10 reloads at less than half the cost of a loaded cassette.

Darkroom refills
The cassette refill can easily be loaded into the cassette by hand, but it must be handled in total darkness. The refill contains a small roll of unspooled film which has to be attached to the spool of the cassette. So, before you unwrap it, dismantle the cassette by removing one end. If your fingernails are not up to this task when re-using film manufacturers' cassettes, rap the protruding end of the spool sharply on a hard flat surface and the end of the cassette will pop off. Lay the spool, cassette shell and cap to hand in front of you in the darkroom or other completely darkened area. You can keep the lights on at this stage, however, while you also cut about two inches of adhesive tape or paper (masking tape is very suitable) with which to fasten the film end of the spool. Few spools nowadays have slots or clips.

Switch off the lights and unwrap the film. Being careful to handle it by the edges only (some people wear thin cotton gloves as an additional precaution) attach the end of the film to the spool with the tape adhering to both sides of the film. Wind the film on to the spool so that, with the protruding end of the spool away from you, the film wraps around the spool in an anti-clockwise direction. If you wind it the other way the film comes out of the cassette when loaded into the camera with the emulsion on the wrong side.

Insert the spool in the cassette shell so that the leader slides down the slot and leaves an inch or two of film protruding. Replace the cassette end cap securely before switching on the lights.

Bulk film loaders
Loading from bulk lengths without special equipment is not so easy because you have to cut off the required length first and return the remainder to its packing. As a 36-exposure length needs more than 5 feet of film, this can be a hazardous procedure. It is a much better idea to obtain a cassette loader.

The loader consists basically of a light-tight container for the roll of film and a cassette chamber with winding handle and counting mechanism. Any length of film can be loaded into a cassette in daylight once the film container has been loaded in darkness.

Loaders vary in complexity and capacity but most common models hold up to 100 feet of film.

Filters and screens

Filters for mounting on camera lenses must be of the highest optical quality. There is no point in buying a specially coated lens accurately made from selected high quality glasses and then fitting over it a filter little better than a piece of window glass. Optical quality gelatin filters are ideal for occasional use, but are too delicate to be used continuously. For constant use glass filters (often a gelatin filter cemented between two pieces of glass) are essential. Filters manufactured for fitting over light sources (either photographic or theatrical) or in colour enlarger heads may produce distorted or degraded pictures if used on the camera. Intentional distortion may be introduced by using a dirty filter, or specially constructed lens attachments and screens. By such means, you can produce blurred images, flare, stars from bright points, multiple images and many other effects. Together with brightly coloured filters, these attachments play an important part in creative photography, but care should be taken to avoid accidentally emulating their effects. You should be specially careful of the condition and quality of a UV filter if, like many photographers, you keep it permanently in place.

Glass filters are supplied in rims which screw into the filter threads on the front of the lenses. The rims are manufactured in a standard range of sizes to suit most lenses. Adapter rings are available to allow the use of larger filters on lenses with smaller filter threads. Because of the standardization, you may be able to use one filter on several lenses, thus justifying the expense of buying a top quality filter.

As filters reduce the light reaching the film, they usually necessitate an increase in exposure time (or lens aperture). This increase is given as the *factor* by which the exposure time should be increased.

Aperture alterations can be calculated from this factor. Thus, for example, a 2× filter requires twice the exposure time or one stop larger aperture etc. Some manufacturers also give exposure increases in *thirds* of a stop. The simplest way of using these with a separate exposure meter (or one built into the camera which uses its own light window) is to decrease the film speed setting by one unit for each $\frac{1}{3}$ stop. Thus a $\frac{2}{3}$ stop increase would need an alteration from 80 ASA (20 DIN) to 50 ASA (18 DIN). Cameras with built-in through-the-lens meters also read through the filter, and thus give the correct exposure without any modification to the film setting. The meter can be used in its normal way.

Filters for black-and-white film

When they are used with black-and-white films UV and polarizing filters reduce haze and reflection respectively, just as they do with colour films. Coloured filters, however, affect the relative tonal rendering of different coloured parts of the subject. Because a filter acts by reducing the passage of light of complementary (opposite) colour, it reduces the image density produced on the negative from an object of that colour. The object thus comes out darker in the final print. If—as is usually the case—the camera exposure is increased to take account of the light absorbed by the filter, objects the same colour as the filter will be rendered lighter than normal in the final print.

The complements of red, green and blue are cyan (blue-green), magenta (red-purple) and yellow respectively; intermediate colours have intermediate complements. From this you can work out the colour of filter you need to give particular emphasis to any part of the subject. Yellow filters are widely used to darken blue parts of the subjects—in particular blue skies to emphasise white clouds.

Without any filter, blue parts of a subject tend to be rendered somewhat lighter than we see them because blue light tends also to contain some ultra-violet radiation, to which the film is sensitive, and the eye is not very sensitive to blue light. For this reason, a medium yellow filter may give a more natural tone rendering on panchromatic film, and is sometimes called a correction filter. The effect may be exaggerated by using a dark yellow or orange filter, or for greatest exaggeration a red filter. Such filters give increasingly darkened skies, with clouds standing out dramatically. The accepted "correction" filter for use with tungsten light is a yellow-green colour.

Because haze tends to reflect blue light and ultra-violet radiation in preference to green or red light, the use of yellow, red or orange filters can reduce its effect on the film. Deep red filters give the strongest haze penetration, but require considerable exposure increase, and of course affect the overall tonal rendering of the photograph.

Neutral density filters, naturally, do not affect the tone rendering. They simply allow you to increase the aperture or lengthen the shutter speed without overexposing the film.

Filters for colour photography

Filters are used in colour photography to alter the colour balance of the image on the film. Their use is mainly confined to reversal films because the colour balance of a print can be determined at the printing stage. Polarizing and ultra-violet absorbing filters, however, are commonly used with negative films as well.

Polarizing filters. The effect of a polarizing filter is the same with all types of film. It can—in some circumstances—reduce reflections; and can darken a blue sky, without otherwise altering the balance in a colour picture.

Light coming directly from the sun or other light source is not polarized: the rays vibrate in all directions. Sometimes, however, light can be restricted to rays all vibrating in one plane. It is then said to be polarized. For the photographer there are two important polarizers: polarizing filters, which restrict the passage of all light not vibrating in their plane of polarization; and smooth reflective non-metallic surfaces which polarize light reflected at certain angles. Although polarizing filters may be fitted over light-sources for special applications, they can normally be regarded as camera fitments used to take advantage of light polarized by reflection.

The most common use is in restricting the passage of polarized light, thus reducing its influence on the film. From certain angles this can result in a dramatic reduction in reflections from glass, water and similar substances (but not from metal surfaces). A special instance of this is the blue light reflected from the sky on a sunny day. An area of the sky at right angles to a line from the sun to the camera position polarises the sun's rays strongly, and thus careful use of a polarizing filter can selectively darken a blue sky in a colour picture.

The effect of a polarizing filter depends on its orientation to the polarized light. It passes almost all light polarized parallel to its polarizing plane, and is opaque to light polarized at right angles.

To simplify their use, polarizing filters for camera use are usually supplied in rotatable mounts. With a single lens reflex camera, you simply view the subject and rotate the filter until you see the effect you want. Some types also have a small extra filter on the rotation handle. This allows you to check the polarizing action independently of the main filter. Polarizing filters require an exposure increase of about $2\frac{1}{2}$ times ($1\frac{1}{3}$ stops).

Ultra-violet filters. Ultra-violet absorbing (UV) filters reduce the effect of atmospheric haze which would otherwise be exaggerated because photographic emulsions are sensitive to ultra-violet radiation (which is invisible to the eye). The radiation is scattered strongly by haze and records on colour film as a blue veiling of distant objects.

113

With colour reversal film an ultra-violet filter has the same haze-cutting effect, and also reduces the blue cast sometimes found in transparencies taken close to large reflecting masses such as water or snow. Such filters require no exposure increase.

Sky-light filters. Skylight filters are ultra-violet absorbing filters coloured a pale salmon or rose. They are used with reversal films to give slightly warmer colours in transparencies, as well as the normal UV filter effects. They require no exposure increase, and are a more useful alternative to plain UV filters.

Colour conversion filters. To obtain a normal colour balance when using a colour reversal film with a light source other than that for which it is intended to be used, you must use a coloured filter. Filters designed for this purpose are known as conversion filters. Many manufacturers supply them for using commonly available film types in normal types of illumination. In general, filters for use with daylight films are blue in colour, and those for use with artificial light films are orange. The filters are normally used on the camera lens, but are equally effective when used to filter the light-source. If you are to use two light sources of different colour temperatures, one of them must be filtered to the colour of the other.

Colour balancing filters. For special effects and for accurate colour matching, it may be necessary to change the colour balance slightly. Manufacturers supply two types of filter which are suitable: special pale filters designed for the purpose, and filters designed for colour printing. Almost invariably the necessity for particular filters can be determined only by testing, and information should be sought from the filter manufacturers.

Neutral density filters. Neutral density filters (or attenuators) reduce equally the transmission of all wavelengths of the visible spectrum. They come in two forms —*photographic silver density*, which is simply accurately exposed and developed film; and *dyed filters*—often using colloidal carbon. Because of its high light-scattering effect, silver density is not suitable for use over the camera lens. Dyed neutral density filters are, however, intended for this purpose, and can be used to produce high quality images.

Neutral density filters do not affect the colour balance whatever film they are used with. They simply allow the lens aperture to be widened, or the shutter speed lengthened, while restricting the exposure to its normal level. They are normally available in a range of densities from 0.1 to 4.0 (transmitting from 80% to 0.01% of the available light) with filter factors varying from just over 1 to 10,000. A density between 1.0 and 2.0 (10%–1% transmission) enables you to use full aperture in bright sun with medium speed films. A density of 3.0 (0.1% transmission) allows exposures up to 30 sec under the same conditions.

Exposure and exposure meters

Cameras have two controls over the amount of light that is allowed to act on the film—the shutter, with variable speeds controlling the time during which the light passes, and the aperture, a variable opening in a diaphragm which controls the intensity. Exposure is thus the product of time and intensity and the photographer's task is to choose a pair of settings which, taking into consideration the speed of the film and the lighting conditions, will produce a correctly exposed picture.

The simplest method of assessing the correct exposure is the rule of thumb which says that bright sunny lighting calls for an aperture of f16 and the shutter speed numerically nearest to the film speed, i.e. 1/125 sec at f16 for a 125 ASA film. For cloudy-bright lighting use f11, overcast f8, heavy cloud f5.6 and dull f4. So, in the overcast conditions an 80 ASA film would need 1/80 sec at f8, which could be achieved with 1/60 at f8 (or a fraction toward f11).

The leaflet packed with the film gives sample exposures generally closely following this rule and if you use the exposures there given, you will not go far wrong. Naturally, you do not have to use the actual settings quoted. Either shutter speed or aperture can be adjusted to suit the subject. The 1/125 sec at f16 we quoted could be altered to 1/500 sec at f8 for a fast-moving subject. This is a shortening of time and increase of intensity that provides the same result.

Typical outdoor exposures—aperture at 1/500 sec.

| Weather Conditions | Film speeds ASA | | | | |
	25–40	50–80	100–160	200–320	400–640
Bright sun* in bright surroundings	5.6	8	11	16	22
Bright or hazy sun	4	5.6	8	11	16
Light overcast	2.8	4	5.6	8	11
Cloudy	2	2.8	4	5.6	8
Dull**	1.4	2	2.8	4	5.6

*White sand, snow, whitewashed buildings, etc.
**Also subjects in the shade on sunny days.
Backlit subjects need about two stops more exposure in harsh lighting conditions.
One hour after sunrise, and one hour before sunset, give one stop more exposure.
In winter months give one stop more exposure.

How exposure meters work

Exposure meters are calibrated to provide the same sort of result but, whereas the rule of thumb or exposure chart cannot be misled by the nature of the subject or lighting, the exposure meter can be. When an exposure meter is used to take a reading from a small subject in a vast expanse of snow or other light-coloured background, it does not indicate 1/125 sec at f16 for a 125 ASA film in bright sunlight. It is more likely to indicate 1/500 sec or less, leading to underexposure. Similarly, a predominantly dark subject may be overexposed if you follow the meter reading. This is because the meter is programmed to believe that everything it sees averages out to a mid-tone. It starts off on the wrong foot when faced with an unusual subject.

This applies equally to separate meters, built-in meters and through-the-lens meters—even the so-called spot type. The meter that reads only a small part of the scene may, in fact, be more easily misled than the meter that reads the whole screen area, because the smaller the area, the less likely that it will contain a variety of tones. The spot metering type needs to be used with extra care.

When you take a meter reading, make sure that you read an area of tones averaging out to grey. If the subject does not contain such an area change the angle of your camera or meter, provided it still measures in the same light conditions. If you cannot find a suitable area or object point the meter at the back of your hand, again positioned in such a way that the light falling on it is the same as that on the subject. The back of the hand is often a reasonable mid-tone, especially for colour photography. This is more or less equivalent to taking a reading from a standard grey card, which is a card reflecting 18% of the light falling on it.

Non-average subjects

The exposure recommendations resulting from this type of reading are suitable for virtually any subject—whatever the lighting, whatever the nature of the subject. That is not to say that it always gives perfect results. If the subject is extremely contrasty—deep shadows and strong highlights—you may lose detail in either shadows or highlights or both. With colour film you will certainly lose colour fidelity at one end or the other. Films can handle accurately only a limited range of brightnesses; subjects with a very long scale of tones receive a compromise exposure which you have to bias toward whichever end of the scale is of most importance. Generally, you tend to underexpose a little to preserve detail and colour accuracy in the highlights but there are times when shadow detail is more important. If both are equally important, you have to bring in supplementary lighting or use reflectors to brighten the shadows and so shorten the scale.

Exposure is not the problem it is so often made out to be and there is a tendency, now that meter readings are so often displayed in the viewfinder, to pay too much attention to it. If you take a careful reading when you first start shooting, there is little reason to take further readings until you have reason to believe that the light has changed. A single, straightforward reading from the subject area may not be absolutely accurate, whereas your original careful reading (preferably from a grey card or substitute) should be quite reliable. To adjust for every shot on the basis of meter needle movement is time-wasting and rather foolish.

Flash equipment

The flashbulb is a glass envelope filled with finely shredded metal or metal foil in an atmosphere of oxygen. Two electrodes (wires) pass through the glass to form contacts outside the envelope to which a voltage can be applied. Current passes through the wires to a primer paste at their other ends (inside the envelope). The current causes the paste to ignite, so firing the metal filling which burns rapidly in an intense flash of light. A great deal of heat is generated and the glass envelope is shattered. The pieces are, however, held together by a heavy varnish on the outside of the envelope.

Flashgun circuitry

Flashbulbs can be fired by very low voltages but they need a high current. The average low-voltage battery could provide this high current reliably only for a very few firings. Consequently, bulb flashguns usually have a capacitor in their power circuit to act as a current store. When a suitable capacitor is connected to a battery, it rapidly charges up to the battery voltage with a relatively low current flow. When the capacitor terminals are connected to a flashbulb, they are effectively short circuited and the capacitor discharges almost instantaneously with a high current flow. While you change the bulb the capacitor charges up again.

Thus, reliability is improved and the necessary high current is always available while the battery lasts.

The flashbulb is, of course, expendable. It can be fired only once. But it comes in many sizes, from tiny bulbs like the AG-3B to the light-bulb sized monsters such as the PF100, with an output more than $12 \times$ greater. The very large bulbs generally have a screw fitting and need to be fired from a larger flashgun but small, pocketable units are adequate for several of the smaller sizes up to the PF5, which has more than double the power of the AG-3B, or special focal plane bulbs such as the PF6.

Bulb flashguns are inexpensive and can be extremely small, with folding reflectors and miniature components, the power unit consisting only of a small battery, capacitor and resistor.

All small flashbulbs are now blue-coated to simulate daylight so that they can be used with daylight colour film. Clear types are available in the larger sizes and are sometimes preferred for negative colour and black-and-white work.

The most significant difference between the flashbulb and the electronic flash tube is that the bulb takes a measurable time to ignite, needing, on average, about 20 milliseconds to reach full brilliance. The usable output of light lasts for 10–20 milliseconds, except with special long-burning focal plane bulbs designed for use with focal plane shutters at the faster speeds.

Synchronisation

The ordinary bulb can be used only at the slower speeds of a focal plane shutter because it is only at those speeds that the film is totally uncovered. At faster speeds the shutter blinds uncover only part of the film at any given moment so that the effect is of a slit travelling across the film. Only the special focal plane bulbs burn long enough to provide even illumination throughout the travel of the shutter blinds.

On all modern cameras, the firing of the flashbulb is synchronised with the shutter opening by contacts in the camera connected to a coaxial socket on the camera body and/or a contact in the accessory shoe (the "hot shoe" contact). All flashguns are provided with a cord to plug into the coaxial (PC) socket, while many have the additional hot shoe contact that needs no cord. Adapters are available to allow cord-only guns to be used on cameras with only a hot-shoe contact.

How electronic flash works

Electronic flash is basically a spark discharge between two electrodes. It relies on the fact that if two electrical conductors are brought close together and a voltage is applied to one of them, current will flow between the two conductors via a spark. Such a simple spark gives very little light, however, so for electronic flash the electrode ends are sealed into a glass tube filled with a suitable gas (usually xenon). A third electrode clamped or wound round the outside of the tube carries a very high current which ionises the gas and lowers its resistance to the spark discharge. By this means the spark can be lengthened and its brilliance enormously enhanced.

Electronic flash tubes are available in a wide variety of shapes and sizes to suit various designs of equipment from the low-power pocketable unit to the large floor-mounted equipment of the professional studio.

The weight and bulk of an electronic flash unit is governed principally by its power unit. The greater the light output required, the bigger and bulkier the power unit, which is basically similar to that of the bulb flashgun but is much more complicated because high voltages are required to fire an electronic flash tube. The trigger voltage needed to ionise the gases in the tube runs to thousands of volts while few tubes need less than 500 volts applied to the internal electrodes.

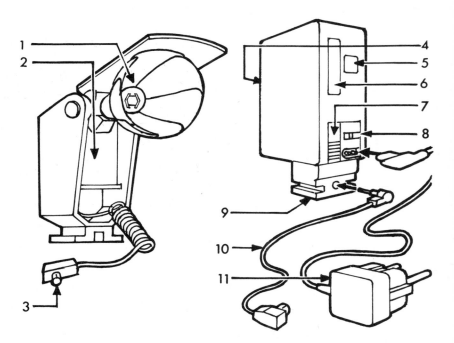

Most bulb flashguns are now very small with folding reflectors. 1, reflector. 2, battery compartment. 3, connecting cable and plug. There are also many relatively small electronic units. 4, flash tube. 5, film speed setting. 6, exposure calculator. 7, ready light. 8, power switch. 9, accessory shoe fitting. 10, connecting cable and plug. 11, charging unit.

Nevertheless the now commonly used transistor circuitry allows small electronic flashguns to operate from built-in rechargeable batteries of 1–1.5 volts. Others use two or four small dry batteries of the traditional type or the newer, high-capacity alkaline type. Many flashguns are also available with the additional facility of working from household current.

The main advantage of electronic flash is that the tube will fire thousands of times before burning out. So no bulb changing is necessary and the cost per flash is minimal over the life of the equipment. The disadvantage is that, weight for weight, the bulb flash can be considerably more powerful. An electronic flash unit able to provide a light output equivalent to that of, say, a PF5, would be very bulky indeed, while nothing short of a really heavy floor-mounted power unit could provide anything approaching the output of the largest flashbulbs.

Nevertheless, even the smaller electronic units can be sufficiently powerful for a variety of uses and they have the added advantage of controllability that comes with automatic operation in the latest models.

Automatic or "computer" flash

The guide number system of flash exposure calculation calls for a certain agility with figures that many people find irksome. Even the calculator discs incorporated in most small electronic flashguns made the necessary calculations only slightly easier. Various semi-automatic methods have been tried by camera manufacturers but the only really simple and fully automatic method applied to the flashgun itself is that of the so-called computer type. The word is here used in its normal sense in that the flash unit circuitry calculates the amount of light needed in given circumstances and terminates the output from the flash tube when that amount of light has been emitted from the tube.

Basically, the procedure is that the light reflects back from the subject to a sensor in the flashgun which, with its allied circuitry, measures the amount of light and switches off the tube when the correct amount of light has been received. Naturally, such units can operate only within the range of their available light output and must be pre-set to take account of the speed of the film in the camera. This is usually achieved by allocating one lens aperture value (f-number) or a limited range of f-numbers for use with each film speed. On a typical small unit, for example, the lens aperture must be set to f 8 or f 5.6 when using a 125 ASA film. A switch on the flashgun is moved to the appropriate position for either of these settings and a third position allows the unit to be used manually in the normal way.

Disadvantages of these units are that they should generally be mounted on or very near to the camera and few of them allow indirect lighting because the light measured by the sensor would in that case be the light from the reflecting surface used to provide the indirect lighting. There are a few units, however, which allow the head to be swivelled independently of the sensor, which can still point at the subject. Again, however, as the sensor should remain close to the camera, the value of such units is limited. Some units can be connected to a separate sensor mounted on the camera.

There are two types of automatic flashgun. In the earlier models, the light not used was diverted through a so-called black tube and was wasted. In later models, this unused power is returned to the power unit capacitor, providing the twin advantages of more flashes per set of batteries or battery recharge and a faster recycling time. Naturally, however, these advantages are considerable only if you carry out a large proportion of ultra close range work calling for short exposures. With colour materials in particular, such methods are not advisable, owing to the possible effects of reciprocity failure.

Flash exposures

Unlike other light sources, a flashbulb or single firing of an electronic flash tube emit a finite, constant and measurable amount of light. In general use the flash is also small enough to be regarded as a point light source, which means that it is subject to the inverse square law—the amount of light reaching the subject is in inverse proportion to the ratio between the squares of the flash-to-subject distances. With the flash at 9 ft the light on the subject is $(3/9)^2$ or one-ninth the strength of the same flash at 3 ft from the subject.

Lens apertures work in a similar way. At $f2$ the light transmitted is $(8/2)^2$ or 16 times the light transmitted at $f8$.

Thus, whenever flash distance and f-number multiplied together give the same result the amount of light reaching the film is the same, i.e. $f2$ and 20 ft, $f4$ and 10 ft, $f8$ and 5 ft etc., because, for example, changing from $f4$ to $f2$ *increases* light transmission fourfold while changing the flash distance from 10 ft to 20 ft *decreases* the light falling on the subject fourfold.

If these factors provided correct exposure, therefore the figure 40 could be ascribed to that particular flash unit as an exposure guide number.

That is how the guide number system works. Every flashbulb and electronic flash unit has guide numbers applicable to various film speeds. Flashbulb packings also quote different guide numbers according to shutter speed but these do not normally apply to focal plane shutters, with which the faster speeds cannot be used. You take the open flash or 1/30 sec number. When using focal plane type bulbs, you should use the guide number for your chosen shutter speed.

To calculate the aperture required for correct exposure, you simply divide the flash distance (not the camera distance, unless the flash is on the camera) into the guide number and round off to the nearest f-number. Alternatively, if you wish to shoot at a particular aperture you divide the f-number into the guide number to find the distance at which you have to place the flash.

If that means that the flash has to be used at a greater distance than that from which you wish to shoot, you can use an extension flash cable, obtainable from any photo dealer.

Typical flash guide numbers (feet/metres)

Flash source	Film speeds (ASA)				
	25–40	50–80	100–160	200–320	400–640
MF Class bulbs					
Small bulbs, magicubes					
flashcubes (Type 1B,					
AG1B, AG3B etc)	60/18	80/24	120/36	160/48	240/72
Medium (Type 5B etc)	100/30	160/48	200/60	320/96	400/120
FP-Class bulbs					
Medium (Type 6B etc)	45/14	65/20	90/27	130/39	180/54
Electronic flash					
Small pocket guns	25/8	40/12	50/15	80/24	100/30
Medium pocket guns	40/12	60/18	80/24	120/36	160/48
Large 'pocket' guns	50/15	70/21	100/30	140/142	200/60
'Professional' type guns	70/21	100/30	140/42	200/60	280/76

Guide numbers for bulbs apply only to shutter speeds of 1/30 second or longer (1/60 with FP bulbs). At shorter speeds the number must be reduced.
Electronic flash guide numbers apply at all suitable speeds.

Using flash

Many modern cameras have an accessory shoe mounted on the pentaprism with a centre flash contact. A cableless flashgun can fit directly into the shoe and make contact with the flash switch linked to the shutter blind movement. Cameras with no built-in accessory shoe can usually be fitted with an attachable type. The flashgun is then plugged in to the appropriate flash socket on the camera.

A flashgun on the camera does not, however, provide a very satisfactory lighting arrangement. It throws harsh shadows on nearby backgrounds and possibly under the nose, chin, hairline, etc. according to the camera position. It provides little or no modelling to features.

A simple solution to these problems is to tilt the flashgun upward or sideways to reflect light back on to the subject from a large surface, which must be white or neutral-coloured if you use colour film. Special accessories for tilting camera-mounted flash units can be obtained from photo dealers.

Whenever possible, it is better to remove the flash unit from the camera and place it to one side on an extension lead. This serves the dual purpose of separating the shadow from the subject, perhaps allowing it to be excluded from the picture area, and at the same time giving some modelling to the features by a greater variation of light and shade.

Using a second flash

Even when off the camera, however, the single flash still throws heavy shadows and, when placed for the best modelling effect, may leave parts of the subject in almost complete shadow. Such shadows can be relieved by placing a reflecting surface, such as a large card, on the other side of the subject so as to throw light back on to it or by using a second flashgun or extension head, where available, at the camera position.

The second flash should be weaker than that used for modelling because its function is to lighten the shadows slightly, not to obliterate them. It should, therefore, be farther away than the main light or should be covered by a layer or two of clean handkerchief. The second flash (plugged into a Y-connector) should preferably be of the same make and model as the first, and the method is not fully recommended owing to the possibility of overloading the flash contacts in the camera. Flash manufacturers can usually supply slave sensors which give the second flash automatically on receiving light from the first.

Flash can also be used as a fill-light in daylight, particularly to relieve the shadows thrown by an unclouded sun. You should preferably take your subject into the shade but where that is not possible, shadows thrown by back or side lighting from the sun can be relieved by a weak frontal flash. When using flash in this way, the guide number for exposure purposes should be at least doubled.

The guide number has to be modified for bounced flash too. The effective flash distance is from flash to reflecting surface and thence to the subject. There may be losses by absorption at the reflecting surface, but these are generally offset by some direct light reaching the subject from the edge of the flash beam.

Where two flashguns or an extension head are used, it is not usually necessary to take any account for exposure of the fill-in flash.

Multiple exposures

For normal purposes, modern cameras will give one exposure—and one exposure only—on each frame of the film. However, deliberate double exposures may be used to record intermingling images, or to enliven an otherwise dull part of a picture.

When two different subjects are to be merged, the total exposure should be more or less correct for the film in use. Thus, to portray a "ghost" on an otherwise bare beach, take a portrait at about 1 stop under-exposed (set exposure factor scale at $\frac{1}{2} \times$, alter aperture to 1 stop smaller or shutter to one speed faster). Reset the shutter, and then under-expose the overall scene by one stop.

Another use is in making title transparencies. The background may be a normally exposed picture. The title is then set up in white letters on a matt black background. This is given a normal exposure (or slight over-exposure) so that the white letters "burn out" to give a white image superimposed on the background.

Bare areas of blue sky may be filled with suitably exposed clouds, but this is not easy without spoiling the rest of the picture. With some acquired skill, however, suns or moons can be added to a scene by double exposure (as long as they are set in an area of blank sky). Remember that the sun in particular must be given the shortest practicable exposure so as to reproduce the sky as nearly black as possible. The sun or moon can be exaggerated in size by using a longer focus lens.

When you need a number of multiply-exposed pictures, you can take one series of exposures, rewind the film, and then take the second series. For example, if you take a reel of background shots out of doors, you can then set up your titling equipment and superimpose titles on them. To do this, the first time you load it, you must mark the film position accurately before you close the camera back. Use a felt-tip pen, either indicating which sprocket holes are on the sprockets, or drawing a line across at the cassette lips. After the first series of exposures, rewind the film but ensure the tongue stays outside the cassette. When you reload the film, make sure it is in exactly the same position when you close the camera back, and then wind it on the same number of times to get back to the first frame.

Few mechanisms for obtaining double exposures can be considered 100% accurate, and allowance should be made wherever possible. For instance, if titles are only half frame width, you can be sure that they will come out complete. If they turn out to be off-centre, the slide can be masked on one side or the other.

Shooting at close range

To enable a lens to focus objects close to it, the distance between the film and the lens needs to be increased. That is what you do when you turn the focusing ring on the average lens. The glass components of the lens move forward in their mounting within the lens barrel. With most lenses the amount of travel thus provided is restricted and the closest focus allowed with the average standard lens barely reaches the true close-up field. A wide angle lens generally focuses closer, while the longer the focal length the more distant the minimum focusing plane.

If you wish to focus at really close range, therefore, you have two alternatives:

1. You can add a lens to the camera lens to shorten its focal length so that the existing travel has a greater effect.
2. You can interpose extension tubes or an extension bellows between lens and camera to increase the separation between camera and film.

Close-up lenses

Close-up lenses are relatively inexpensive, usually single-glass constructions in filter-type mounts to attach to the front of the camera lens. They are rated in dioptres, indirectly indicating the focal length, which is the dioptre number divided into one metre. Thus a 1-dioptre lens has a focal length of one metre or $39\frac{1}{4}$ in; the focal length of a 3-dioptre lens is 30 cm or about 13 in. Strengths above 3 dioptres are less common and generally need to be of higher quality and price.

With the camera lens set to infinity you can focus objects at a distance equal to the focal length of the close-up lens, measured from the front of the lens. The normal focusing travel allows a restricted range of closer focusing.

Exposure is not affected by the close-up lens. There is no increase in lens extension so the aperture values remain as in normal photography.

Extension tubes and bellows

Extension tubes are, exactly as their name implies, metal rings or tubes to provide a fixed amount of additional distance between lens and film. They are usually supplied in sets of three, typical values being 7, 14 and 28 mm. Automatic types are now available for most reflex cameras, connecting the auto-diaphragm mechanisms of camera body and lens.

Extension bellows perform the same function but allow variable extension between the limits of the bellows length and the minimum extension provided by the front and rear standards and the fully compressed bellows. Automatic diaphragm facilities are not generally available with bellows except by an external linkage or the use of a double cable release.

Exposure factors

As the function of extension tubes and bellows is to increase the distance between lens and film and therefore the distance the image-forming rays have to travel, there is a loss of light intensity at the film surface. This means that the lens f-numbers do not give an accurate impression of the exposure effect. Rather than adjust the f-number for each degree of extension, however, it is easier to use an exposure factor calculated from $(E/F)^2$, where E = total extension, i.e. focal length plus additional extension provided by bellows or tubes, and F = focal length of the camera lens. Thus, when 7 mm and 28 mm extension tubes are used together on a 50 mm lens, the exposure factor is $(85/50)^2 = 2.89$. The normally calculated exposure should thus be increased threefold, i.e. open up the lens by $1\frac{1}{2}$ stops. No such calculation is necessary, however, where the camera has a through-the-lens meter.

Close-up depth of field

Aperture f	Depth of field in inches for scale of reproduction						
	0·1 (1 : 10)	0·17 (1 : 6)	0·25 (1 : 4)	0·5 (1 : 2)	1 (1 : 1)	2 (2 : 1)	3 (3 : 1)
2	0·22	0·084	0·040	0·012	0·0040	0·0015	0·0009
2·8	0·31	0·12	0·056	0·017	0·0056	0·0021	0·0012
4	0·44	0·17	0·080	0·024	0·0080	0·0030	0·0018
5·6	0·62	0·23	0·11	0·034	0·011	0·0042	0·0025
8	0·88	0·34	0·16	0·048	0·016	0·0060	0·0036
11	1·21	0·46	0·22	0·066	0·022	0·0082	0·0049
16	1·76	0·67	0·32	0·096	0·032	0·012	0·0071
22	2·42	0·92	0·44	0·13	0·044	0·016	0·0098
32	3·5	1·34	0·64	0·19	0·064	0·024	0·014
45	4·9	1·90	0·90	0·27	0·090	0·034	0·020

Aperture f	Depth of field in millimetres for scale of reproduction						
	0·1 (1 : 10)	0·17 (1 : 6)	0·25 (1 : 4)	0·5 (1 : 2)	1 (1 : 1)	2 (2 : 1)	3 (3 : 1)
2	5·5	2·10	1·00	0·30	0·10	0·038	0·022
2·8	7·7	2·94	1·40	0·42	0·14	0·052	0·031
4	11·0	4·2	2·00	0·60	0·20	0·775	0·044
5·6	15·4	5·9	2·80	0·84	0·28	0·10	0·062
8	22·0	8·4	4·0	1·20	0·40	0·15	0·089
11	30	11·5	5·5	1·65	0·55	0·21	0·12
16	44	16·8	8·0	2·40	0·80	0·30	0·18
22	60	23·1	11·0	3·3	1·10	0·41	0·24
32	88	34	16·0	4·8	1·60	0·60	0·36
45	124	47	22·5	6·7	2·25	0·84	0·50

Circle of confusion 0·001 in/0·025 mm. The depth of field shown is at each side of the plane of sharp focus. The total depth is twice these figures.

Working methods

Important points to bear in mind when working at close range is that depth of field is extremely shallow and perspective distortion of three-dimensional objects is inevitable. You can reduce the perspective distortion by shooting from a greater distance with a longer focus lens but you can do little about the reduced depth of field beyond focusing precisely on the plane of most importance and stopping down as far as possible.

In most set-ups, a tripod is essential, because of the requirement for accurate focusing. It is quite possible to hand-hold, however, when using very little extra extension on longer focus lenses to shoot, for example, wild flowers or plants. You may well be able to use a small flashgun on such occasions and shoot at small apertures.

Tele-extenders can be used in close-range work to magnify the image without moving closer and risking perspective distortion. In static set-ups, the light loss is rarely of great importance.

Interchangeable lenses

One of the major reasons for buying a system camera, particularly a single-lens reflex, is to enable you to choose the lens to suit the picture. The most important feature of a lens is its angle of view. For any given format, this is directly related to its focal length. The angle of view is normally measured across the diagonal of the format. The angles of view of normal lenses for 35 mm cameras vary from about 110° to 1°. The quoted angles of view for really short focus lenses (less than 20 mm) tend to vary from one manufacturer to another, partly because slight variations in actual focal length greatly affect the angles and partly because of differing measurement techniques. The only way to determine whether a lens is suited to your purpose is to test it on your camera.

Different focal lengths

Choosing the focal length—and thus the angle of view—of a lens allows you to choose the area of a scene you include from a particular viewpoint. Wide-angle lenses allow you to include a broad sweep in one picture, whereas long-focus (narrow-angle) lenses allow you to concentrate on one small part—thus magnifying a distant object. If you can alter your viewpoint, altering the focal length allows you to vary the perspective in your picture while still showing the important part of your subject the same size. Another reason for changing from one lens to another is to change the depth of field while maintaining a usable *f*-number.

Although individual photographers tend to regard other lenses as their standard, most 35 mm cameras are supplied with a lens of between 45 and 55 mm. These

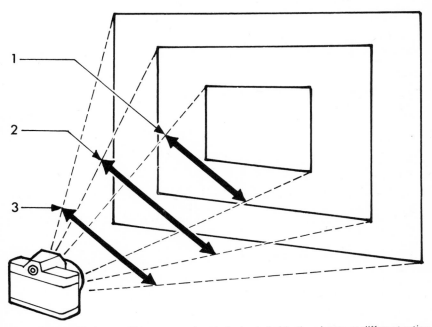

Interchangeable lenses allow more or less to be included in the picture at different ratios of reproduction. 1, *long-focus.* 2, *standard.* 3, *wide-angle.*

lenses approximate to the angle of view of the human eye (50–43°), and so under most circumstances produce pictures with pleasing perspective (when they are viewed from a "normal" distance). Some photographers advocate wider angles, such as 55–62° (40–35 mm), whereas others prefer to take most of their pictures with an 85 or 90 mm lens giving an angle of about 27 or 28°, so the 45–55 mm seems to be a good compromise.

Long-focus lenses

Most non-photographers immediately assume that extra lenses are telephoto lenses, because some of their attributes are obvious. They allow the user to take photos of distant subjects, or to isolate the important parts of a scene. Telephoto lenses are, in fact, long-focus lenses which have a physical length shorter than their focal length, and they behave in exactly the same way as ordinary long-focus lenses of the same focal length. They are, however, smaller and lighter.

Moderately long-focus lenses—about 85 to 150 mm—have two functions. They magnify parts of the subject too distant to be pictured with the standard lens and allow the photographer to use a viewpoint which gives pleasing perspective in portraits. These two features combine to make them excellent lenses for taking pictures of children playing or of relatively unsuspecting adults. Lenses from 80 to 105 mm are usually regarded as optimum for normal portrait work.

Longer-focus lenses are useful for sports or nature photography, as they give quite large images even when you cannot get near the subject. Because they also magnify the effects of subject or camera movement, however, they need some care in handling, and lenses longer than 300 mm focal length are unlikely to give their best performance without a firm support.

Shooting from a distance has the effect of compressing the perspective of the final picture. This is purely an effect of magnifying part of the scene, as may be seen by enlarging a small sector from a negative taken with the standard lens, but the "crowding" effect should be remembered when composing your picture. You can use the effect, for example, to picture an enormous moon apparently just behind a close-up of a tree, which was actually some distance from the camera.

Wide-angle lenses

For many photographers, the first accessory lens is a wide-angle. Wide-angle lenses for single lens reflex cameras are normally of reversed telephoto construction. This construction allows them to focus an image on the film from a distance greater than their focal length, thus allowing room for the mirror to move up and down.

The most popular wide-angle lens has long been the 35 mm, but 30 or 28 mm lenses are becoming much more widely used. Such wide angle lenses allow you to get more in a picture without moving back further, and are particularly useful when shooting in confined spaces. One particular use is to take pictures of tall buildings, without the converging verticals which would be caused if you were to tilt the camera to include the top.

The other important feature of wide-angle lenses is their great depth of field. Careful use can give pictures in which the whole subject is sharp from a few feet to infinity. Such pictures, however, often show "wide-angle distortion" because of the close viewpoint needed to picture objects at a large size. The effect is often used creatively, but wide-angle lenses—especially extreme ones of 24 mm or less—must be treated with respect if this effect is not to spoil your normal pictures.

Time exposures

For many years after the introduction of photography, the standard exposures were several seconds, or even minutes, long. Portraits were taken with the subjects sitting rigidly still, their heads firmly supported by a neck clamp. Today such long exposures—usually called time exposures—are necessary only in very low light levels or for special effects.

Time exposures may be needed for taking photographs indoors by the existing light, or outdoors after dark. Occasionally, under normal lighting conditions, a time exposure may be needed to allow a small lens aperture to give maximum depth of field. Very long time exposures may be used to picture a scene which would otherwise be marred by transitory objects or people. For example, as long as none of them stay still for much of the time a 30 min exposure in a public square could produce a picture devoid of any signs of people passing through. Even with a slow film, to avoid over-exposure, such a picture would require a dense neutral density filter over the camera lens. In darkened conditions, time exposures may be used to record moving lights, such as fireworks or stars, as streaks on the film.

Whenever the exposure is longer than 1/30 sec, the camera must be firmly supported, preferably on a tripod or other specially designed camera stand. Care must be taken to avoid shaking the camera, and it is best to use a cable release to trip the shutter.

The range of mechanically timed shutter speeds is limited by the construction of the shutter mechanism. You can make longer exposures by using the B (brief time or bulb) setting. On this setting, the shutter remains open as long as the shutter button is depressed. If you use a locking cable release, the shutter can be locked open at the beginning of the exposure and will not close until the cable release is unlocked. This is useful for exposures longer than half a minute, and essential—unless you can lock the shutter button down—for much longer exposures. A number of accessory manufacturers supply timers which give accurately timed exposures when used on the B setting. Some of these have a built-in delay to allow vibrations to die down.

If you can lock down the shutter button—or arrange for it to be held down with sticky tape, it is possible to use long exposure times without a cable release. The camera must be set up to take the photo and firmly supported. While the button is being pressed and locked—or stuck—down, you prevent light reaching the film by holding a matt black object just in front of the lens. The lens cap could be used, but must be positioned accurately so that it excludes all light without actually touching the lens mount. You then allow all vibrations to die away, and make the exposure by letting the light reach the lens, finishing by re-covering it. If you use the lens cap, it can now be pushed securely into place. Mechanically timed exposures, which would normally need a cable release, can be made using a self-timer (either built-in or as an accessory) to release the shutter. This allows the camera to become quite still before opening the shutter.

Exposure calculations

It is difficult to calculate the exact exposure needed because film emulsions react unusually to long exposure times. This is especially marked with colour films, many of which produce progressively worse colour balance as the exposure times increase over about one second. For optimum results, you should take several pictures "bracketing" your calculated exposure by at least two stops either way. Although your meter may well not give you the exposure time directly, you may be able to calculate it from readings taken at wider apertures, or with a higher film speed.

Depth of field

In theory, a lens placed at a given distance from the image plane (the film) produces a sharp image of objects in a single plane at a certain distance in front of the lens. Objects in front of or behind that plane are rendered less sharply.

In practice, each image point formed by a lens is, in fact, a disc of finite size and, up to a certain degree of enlargement for a given viewing distance, the difference between the smallest possible disc and various slightly larger discs is indistinguishable to the human eye. The relative sizes of the various discs or image points formed by a lens can be envisaged by regarding the light reflected from the point and concentrated by the lens as a solid cone, with the effective aperture of the lens as its base. Thus, when the aperture is small and/or the lens-to-subject distance is large, the cone is relatively slender. At its apex (the crossover point for objects behind the focused plane), there is a relatively deep zone both fore and aft in which the discs formed by a section through the cone are still small enough to be rendered as discs indistinguishable from points on the film and, indeed, on considerably enlarged images.

This zone is the depth of field. As our explanation implies, it is greater when the effective lens aperture is smaller and when the focused distance is greater.

Enlargement and viewing distance

A complication arises with the comparatively small negative or slide sizes used today. Most final images, whether prints or projected slides, are considerably larger than the images produced on the film. Moreover, many prints are made from only part of the negative image and the degree of enlargement is not proportional to the print size. But most final images are viewed from a distance appropriate to their size, not, as they ideally should be, to their degree of enlargement. The complication then is that detail which looks sharp when enlarged less or viewed from a greater distance looks distinctly less sharp when enlarged to a greater degree or viewed from closer range.

Depth of field formulae and tables, therefore, must always be regarded as approximations. Although it is possible to make exact mathematical calculations based on focal length, f-number, focused distance and the size of the acceptable disc (known in this context as the circle of confusion), it is self-evident that you do not produce a sharp image of an object at 10.1 metres and an unsharp image of an object at 10.11 or even 10.2 metres. Depending on the use you wish to make of depth of field or the lack of it, you should always use at least a stop smaller or larger than calculators, indicators or tables recommend.

Changing the focused distance

In many cases, you can manipulate depth of field by changing your focused distance. When you want to throw the background out of focus, for example, you can focus forward a little, so that the subject is within the depth of field but the background is well behind it. The opposite also applies. If you focus slightly beyond the subject you extend the zone of sharpness behind it.

When you wish to obtain the greatest depth of field at any given aperture you set the focus at the hyperfocal distance for that aperture. This distance can be calculated or looked up in tables but the easiest method is to set the lens distance scale so that the infinity marking is opposite the f-number at which you are shooting on the depth of field scale. You are then focused at the hyperfocal distance and the depth of field stretches from half that distance to infinity.

Glossary

Aberration. Failing in the ability of a lens to produce a true image. There are many forms of aberration and the lens designer can often correct some only by allowing others to remain. Generally, the more expensive the lens, the less its aberrations.

Angle of view. The extent of the view taken in by a lens. For any particular film size, it varies with the focal length of the lens. Usually expressed on the diagonal of the image area.

Aperture. The opening in the lens, usually provided by an adjustable iris diaphragm, though which light passes. See Limiting aperture, Effective aperture, f-number.

Aperture priority. Automatic exposure system in which the lens aperture is set by the photographer, and the camera sets the shutter speed. Can be used in the stop-down mode with any lens that does not interfere with the metering system.

Artificial light. Light from a man-made source, usually restricted to studio, photolamp and domestic lighting. When used to describe film (also known as Type A or Type B) invariably means these types of lighting.

ASA. Film speed rating defined by the American National Standards Institute.

Automatic iris. Lens diaphragm which is controlled by a mechanism in the camera body coupled to the shutter release. The diaphragm closes to any preset value before the shutter opens and returns to the fully open position when the shutter closes.

Balanced. Description applied to colour films to indicate their ability to produce acceptable colour response in various types of lighting. The films normally available are balanced for daylight (5500–6000K), photolamps (3400K) or studio lamps (3200K).

Cadmium sulphide (CdS). Photo conductive material used in exposure meters as alternative to selenium-based or silicon blue photocells. Its electrical resistance decreases as the light falling on it increases. Cds meters use current from an external power source, such as a battery.

Camera shake. Movement of camera caused by unsteady hold or support, vibration, etc., leading, particularly at slower shutter speeds, to a blurred image on the film. It is a major cause of unsharp pictures, especially with long focus lenses.

Capacitor. Electrical component once more commonly known as a condenser. Stores electrical energy supplied by a power source and can discharge it more rapidly than the source itself. Used in flash equipment, providing reliable bulb firing even from weak batteries, and supplying the surge needed for electronic flash tubes.

Cassette. Light-trapped film container used with 35 mm cameras.

Cast. Abnormal colouring of an image produced by departure from recommended exposure or processing conditions with a transparency film, or when making a colour print. Can also be caused by reflection within the subject as from a hat on to the face.

Click stop. Ball bearing and recess or similar construction used to enable shutter speeds, aperture values, etc. to be set by touch.

Colour negative. Film designed to produce colour image with both tones and colours reversed for subsequent printing to a positive image, usually on paper.

Colour reversal. Film designed to produce a normal colour positive image on the film exposed in the camera for subsequent viewing by transmitted light or projection on to a screen.

Colour temperature. Description of the colour of a light-source by comparing it with the colour of light emitted by a (theoretical) perfect radiator at a particular temperature expressed in kelvins (K). Thus "photographic daylight" has a colour temperature of about 5500K. Photographic tungsten lights have colour temperatures of either 3400K or 3200K depending on their construction.

Component. Part of a compound lens consisting of one element (single lens) or more than one element cemented or otherwise joined together. A lens may therefore be described as 4-element, 3-component when two of the elements are cemented together.

Computer flash. Electronic flash guns which sense the light reflected from the subject, and cut off their output when they have received sufficient light for correct exposure. Most units must be used on or close to the camera for direct lighting only. and the camera lens must be set to a specific aperture (or a small range of apertures) determined by the speed of the film in use.

Condenser. Generally a simple lens used to collect light and concentrate it on a particular area, as in enlarger or projector. Frequently in the form of two plano-convex lenses in a metal housing. A condenser, normally of the fresnel type, is used to ensure even illumination of the viewing screens on SLR cameras.

Contrast. Tonal difference. More often used to compare original and reproduction. A negative may be said to be contrasty if it shows fewer, more widely spaced tones than in the original.

Delayed action. Mechanism delaying the opening of the shutter for some seconds after the release has been operated. Also known as self-timer.

Depth of field. The distance between the nearest and farthest planes in a scene that a lens can reproduce with acceptable sharpness. Varies with effective aperture (and thus with focal length at any particular f-number) focused distance and the standards set for acceptable sharpness.

Developer. Solution used to make visible the image produced by allowing light to fall on the light-sensitive material. The basic constituent is a developing agent which reduces the light-struck silver halide to metallic silver. Colour developers include chemicals which produce coloured dyes coincidentally with reduction of the silver halides.

Diaphragm. Device consisting of thin overlapping metal leaves pivoting outwards to form a circular opening of variable size. Used to control light transmission through a lens.

DIN. Film speed rating defined by the Deutscher Normenausschuss (German standards organisation).

Effective aperture. The diameter of the bundle of light rays striking the first lens element that actually pass through the lens at any given diaphragm setting.

Electronic flash. Light source based on electrical discharge across two electrodes in a gas-filled tube. Usually designed to provide light approximating to daylight.

Element. Single lens used in association with others to form a compound construction.

Emulsion. Suspension of light-sensitive silver salts in gelatin.

Exposure. The act of allowing light to reach the light-sensitive emulsion of the photographic material. Also refers to the amount (duration and intensity) of light which reaches the film.

Exposure factor. A figure by which the exposure indicated for an average subject and/or processing should be multiplied to allow for non-average conditions. Usually applied to filters, occasionally to lighting, processing, etc. Not normally used with through-the-lens exposure meters.

Exposure meter. Instrument containing light sensitive substance which indicates aperture and shutter speed settings required.

Extension bellows. Device used to provide the additional separation between lens and film required for close-up photography. Consists of extendible bellows and mounting plates at front and rear to fit the lens and camera body respectively.

Extension tubes. Metal tubes used to obtain the additional separation between lens and film for close-up photography. They are fitted with screw thread or bayonet mounts to suit various lens mounts.

f-number. Numerical expression of the light-transmitting power of a lens. Calculated from the focal length of the lens divided by the diameter of the bundle of light rays entering the lens and passing through the aperture in the iris diaphragm.

Film base. Flexible support on which light sensitive emulsion is coated.

Filter. A piece of material which restricts the transmission of radiation. Generally coloured to absorb light of certain colours. Can be used over light sources or over the camera lens. Camera lens filters are usually glass—either dyed or sandwiching a piece of gelatin—in a screw-in filter holder.

Fisheye lens. Ultra-wide angle lens giving 180 angle of view. Basically produces a circular image—on 35 mm, 5–9 mm lenses showing whole image, 15–17 mm lenses giving a rectangular image fitting just inside the circle, thus representing 180 across the diagonal.

Fixer. Solution, usually based on sodium thiosulphate, in which films or prints are immersed after development to convert the unexposed silver halides in the emulsion to soluble products that can be washed out. This prevents subsequent deterioration of the image.

Flashbulb. Light source based on ignition of combustible metal wire in a gas-filled transparent envelope. Popular sizes are usually blue-coated to give light approximating to daylight.

Flashcube. Self-contained unit comprising four small flashbulbs with own reflectors. Designed to rotate in special camera socket as film is wound on. Can be used in a special adapter on cameras without the socket, but will not rotate automatically.

Focal length. Distance from a lens to the image it produces of a very distant subject. With a compound lens the point from which it is measured depends on the construction of the lens. It is within the lens with those of normal construction, but may be in front of telephoto lenses, or behind inverted telephotos. Whatever the lens construction, the focal length determines the size of the image formed.

Focus. Generally, the act of adjusting a lens to produce a sharp image. In a camera, this is effected by moving the lens bodily towards or away from the film or by moving the front part of the lens towards or away from the rear part, thus altering its focal length.

Format. Shape and size of image provided by camera or presented in final print or transparency. Governed in the camera by the opening at the rear of the body over which the film passes or is placed. The standard 35 mm format is 36×24 mm; half-frame, 18×24 mm; 126 size, 28×28 mm; 110, 17×13 mm; standard rollfilm (120 size), $2\frac{1}{4} \times 2\frac{1}{4}$ in.

Fresnel. Pattern of a special form of condenser lens consisting of a series of concentric stepped rings, each being a section of a convex surface which would, if continued, form a much thicker lens. Used on focusing screens to distribute image brightness evenly over the screen.

Full aperture metering. TTL metering systems in which the camera simulates the effect of stopping down the lens when the aperture ring is turned, while leaving the diaphragm at full aperture to give full focusing screen brilliance. The meter must be "programmed" with the actual full aperture, and the diaphragm ring setting.

Grain. Minute metallic silver deposit, forming in quantity the photographic image. The individual grain is never visible, even in an enlargement, but the random nature of their distribution in the emulsion causes over-lapping, or clumping, which can lead to graininess in the final image.

Graininess. Visible evidence of the granular structure of a photographic reproduction. Influenced by exposure, development, contrast characteristics and surface of printing paper, emulsion structure and degree of enlargement. Basically increases with increasing film speed.

Grey card. Tone used as representative of mid-tone of average subject. The standard grey card reflects 18 per cent of the light falling on it.

Guide number. Figure allocated to a light source, usually flash, representing the product of aperture number and light-to-subject distance required for correct exposure.

Halation. The production of "halos" round bright spots in an image, by light reflecting from the back of the film-base. General film bases are given a light-absorbing coat—the anti-halation back—to prevent this.

Highlight. Small, very bright part of image or object. Highlights should generally be pure white, although the term is sometimes used to describe the lightest tones of a picture, which, in that case, may need to contain some detail.

Image. Two-dimensional reproduction of a subject formed by a lens. When formed on a surface, i.e. a ground-glass screen, it is a real image; if in space, i.e. when the screen is removed, it is an aerial image. The image seen through a telescope, optical viewfinder, etc. cannot be focused on a surface without the aid of another optical system and is a virtual image.

Incident light. Light falling on a surface as opposed to the light reflected by it.

Infinity. Infinite distance. In practice, a distance so great that any object at that distance will be reproduced sharply if the lens is set at its infinity position, i.e. one focal length from the film.

Interchangeable lens. Lens designed to be readily attached to and detached from a camera.

Inverted telephoto lens. Lens constructed so that the back focus (distance from rear of lens to film) is greater than the focal length of the lens. This construction allows room for mirror movement when short focus lenses are fitted to SLR cameras.

Iris. Strictly, iris diaphragm. Device consisting of thin overlapping metal leaves pivoting outwards to form a circular opening of variable size to control light transmission through a lens.

Leader. Part of film attached to camera take-up spool. 35 mm film usually has a leader of the shape originally designed for bottom-loading Leica cameras, although most cameras simply need a short taper.

Lighting ratio. The ratio of the brightness of light falling on the subject from the main (key) light and other (fill) lights. A ratio of about 3:1 is normal for colour photography, greater ratios may be used for effect in black-and-white work.

Limiting aperture. The actual size of the aperture formed by the iris diaphragm at any setting. Determines, but usually differs from, the effective aperture.

Long-focus. Lens of relatively long focal length designed to provide a narrower angle of view than the normal or standard lens, which generally has an angle of view, expressed on the diagonal of the film format, of about 45 deg. The long focus lens thus takes in less of the view in front of it but on an enlarged scale.

Magicube. Special form of flashcube which is fired by mechanical (not electrical) means. Can be used only on cameras fitted with the appropriate socket.

Manual iris. Diaphragm controlled directly by a calibrated ring on the lens barrel.

Microprism. Minute glass or plastic structure of multiple prisms set in a viewfinder screen to act as a focusing aid. Breaks up an out-of-focus subject into a shimmer but images a focused subject clearly. Will not work satisfactorily at lens apertures smaller than f 5·6.

Mirror lens. Lens in which some (usually two) of the elements are curved mirrors. This construction produces comparatively lightweight short fat long focus lenses. They cannot be fitted with a normal diaphragm.

Modelling. Representation by lighting of the three-dimensional nature of an original in a two-dimensional reproduction.

Neutral density filter. Grey filter that absorbs light of all colours equally and thus has no effect on colour rendering with colour film or tonal values with black and white film. Primarily used with mirror lenses or to enable large apertures to be used in bright light conditions.

Parallax. Apparent change in position of an object due to changed viewpoint. In a camera with separate viewfinder, the taking lens and the viewfinder view an object from slightly different positions. At close range, the image produced on the film is significantly different from that seen in the viewfinder. Completely eliminated in single-lens reflex cameras.

Perspective. Size, position and distance relationship between objects. Varies according to viewpoint so that objects at different distances from the observer appear to be closer together with increasing distance. Thus, a long-focus lens used at long range and a wide-angle lens used very close up provide images very different from that of the standard lens used at a normal working distance.

Photolamp (3400K). Photographic lamp giving more light than a normal lamp of the same wattage, at the expense of filament life. Often referred to by the trade mark Photoflood. Are used with type A colour films.

Plane. Level surface. Used in photography chiefly in respect to focal plane, an imaginary level surface perpendicular to the lens axis in which the lens is intended to form an image. When the camera is loaded the focal plane is occupied by the film surface.

Polarized light. Light waves vibrating in one plane only as opposed to the multi-directional vibrations of normal rays. Natural effect produced by some reflecting surfaces, such as glass, water, polished wood, etc., but can also be simulated by placing a special screen in front of the light source. The transmission of polarized light is restricted by using a screen at an angle to the plane of polarization.

Preset iris. Diaphragm with two setting rings or one ring that can be moved to two positions. One is click-stopped, but does not affect the iris, the other moves freely and alters the aperture. The required aperture is preset on the first ring, and the iris closed down with the second just before exposure.

Rangefinder. Instrument for measuring distances from a given point, usually based on slightly separated views of the scene provided by mirrors or prisms. May be built into non-reflex cameras. Single-lens reflexes may have prismatic range-finders built into their focusing screens.

Refill. Length of film usually for loading into 35 mm cassettes in total darkness. Daylight refills are not now generally available.

Relative aperture. Numerical expression of effective aperture, also known as f-number. Obtained by dividing focal length by diameter of effective aperture.

Resolution. Ability of film, lens or both in conjunction to reproduce fine detail. Commonly measured in lines per millimetre as ascertained by photographing, or focusing the lens on, a specially constructed test target. The resolution of modern lenses and films is so high that differences have no bearing on normal photography except with the simplest lenses and fastest films.

Safelight. Light source consisting of housing, lamp and screen of a colour that will not affect the photographic material in use. Safelight screens are available in various colours and sizes for specific applications.

Scale. Focusing method consisting of set of marks to indicate distances at which a lens is focused. May be engraved around the lens barrel, on the focusing control or on the camera body.

Screen. In a camera, the surface upon which the lens projects an image for viewfinding and, usually, focusing purposes. In SLR cameras, almost universally a fresnel screen with a fine-ground surface. Often incorporates a microprism or split-image rangefinder.

Selenium. Light-sensitive substance which, when used in a barrier-layer construction, generates electrical current when exposed to light. Used in exposure meters. Needs no external power supply.

Self-timer. Mechanism delaying the opening of the shutter for some seconds after the release has been operated. Also known as delayed action.

Semi-automatic iris. Diaphragm mechanism which closes down to the taking aperture when the shutter is released, but must be manually re-opened to full aperture.

Sensitivity. Expression of the nature of a photographic emulsion's response to light. Can be concerned with degree of sensitivity as expressed by film speed or response to light of various colours (spectral sensitivity).

Sharpness. Clarity of the photographic image in terms of focus and contrast. Largely subjective but can be measured to some extent by assessing adjacency effects, i.e. the abruptness of the change in density between adjoining areas of different tone value.

Short-focus. Lens of relatively short focal length designed to provide a wider angle of view than the normal or standard lens, which generally has an angle of view, expressed on the diagonal of the film format, of about 45 deg. The short focus lens takes in more of the view in front of it but on a smaller scale.

Shutter priority. Automatic exposure systems in which the shutter speed is set by the photographer, and the camera selects the lens aperture appropriate to the film speed and the light reflected from the subject. Such systems must meter the light at full aperture and use specially connected lenses.

Silicon. Light-sensitive substance which generates a minute current when exposed to light. Requires no external power source, but, in exposure meters, uses an externally powered amplifier.

Split-image. Form of rangefinder image, bisected so that the two halves of the image are aligned only when the correct object distance is set on the instrument or, in the case of a coupled rangefinder, when the lens is correctly focused. SLR cameras may have a prismatic split-image system in their viewing screen. Works on the same principle as a microprism, and is restricted to apertures of f 5·6 or greater.

Stabilizer. Alternative to fixer where permanence is not required. Used in automatic processing machines and can now provide prints that will not deteriorate noticeably over many months if kept away from strong light.

Stop-down metering. TTL metering in which the light is measured at the picture-taking aperture. As the meter just measures the light passing through the lens, there is no need for any lens-camera interconnections.

Studio lamps (3200K). Tungsten or tungsten halogen lamps designed for studio use. Have a longer life than photolamps, but a lower specific output and colour temperature. Are used with type B films.

Supplementary lens. Generally a simple positive (converging) lens used in front of the camera lens to enable it to focus at close range. The effect is to provide a lens of shorter focal length without altering the lens-film separation, thus giving the extra extension required for close focusing.

Synchronisation. Concerted action of shutter opening and closing of electrical contacts to fire a flashbulb or electronic flash at the correct moment to make most efficient use of the light output. Roughly speaking, FP or M-synchronisation is constructed to fire flashbulbs just before the shutter is fully open, allowing a build-up time, and X-synchronisation fires electronic flash exactly at the moment the shutter is fully open.

Telephoto. Special form of long-focus lens construction in which the back focus (distance from rear of lens to film) is much less than the focal length of the lens.

Through-the-lens (TTL). Type of exposure meter built into the camera body and reading through the camera lens. May measure either at full aperture or at picture taking aperture.

Type A. Colour film balanced for use with photolamps (3400K).

Type B. Colour film balanced for use with studio lamps (3200K).

Ultra-wide angle lens. Extra-wide angle lens, usually those with an angle of view greater than 90°. For 35 mm cameras the description usually applies to lenses of shorter focal length than about 24 mm.

Variable focus lens. Lens of which the focal length can be continuously varied between set limits. The lens must be refocused with each change in focal length.

Viewfinder. Device or system indicating the field of view encompassed by the camera lens. The term is sometimes used as a description of the type of camera that does not use reflex or "straight-through" viewing systems and therefore has to have a separate viewfinder.

Vignetting. Underexposure of image corners produced deliberately by shading or unintentionally by inappropriate equipment, such as unsuitable lens hood or badly designed lens. A common fault of wide-angle lenses, owing to reflection, cut-off, etc. of some of the very oblique rays. May be caused in some long-focus lenses by the length of the lens barrel.

Wide-angle. Lens designed to provide a wider angle of view than the normal or standard lens. Generally has an angle of view, expressed on the diagonal of the film format, of about 60 deg. or more. The wide-angle lens thus takes in more of the view in front of it but on a reduced scale.

Zoom lens. Lens of which the focal length can be continuously varied within stated limits while maintaining the focus originally set.